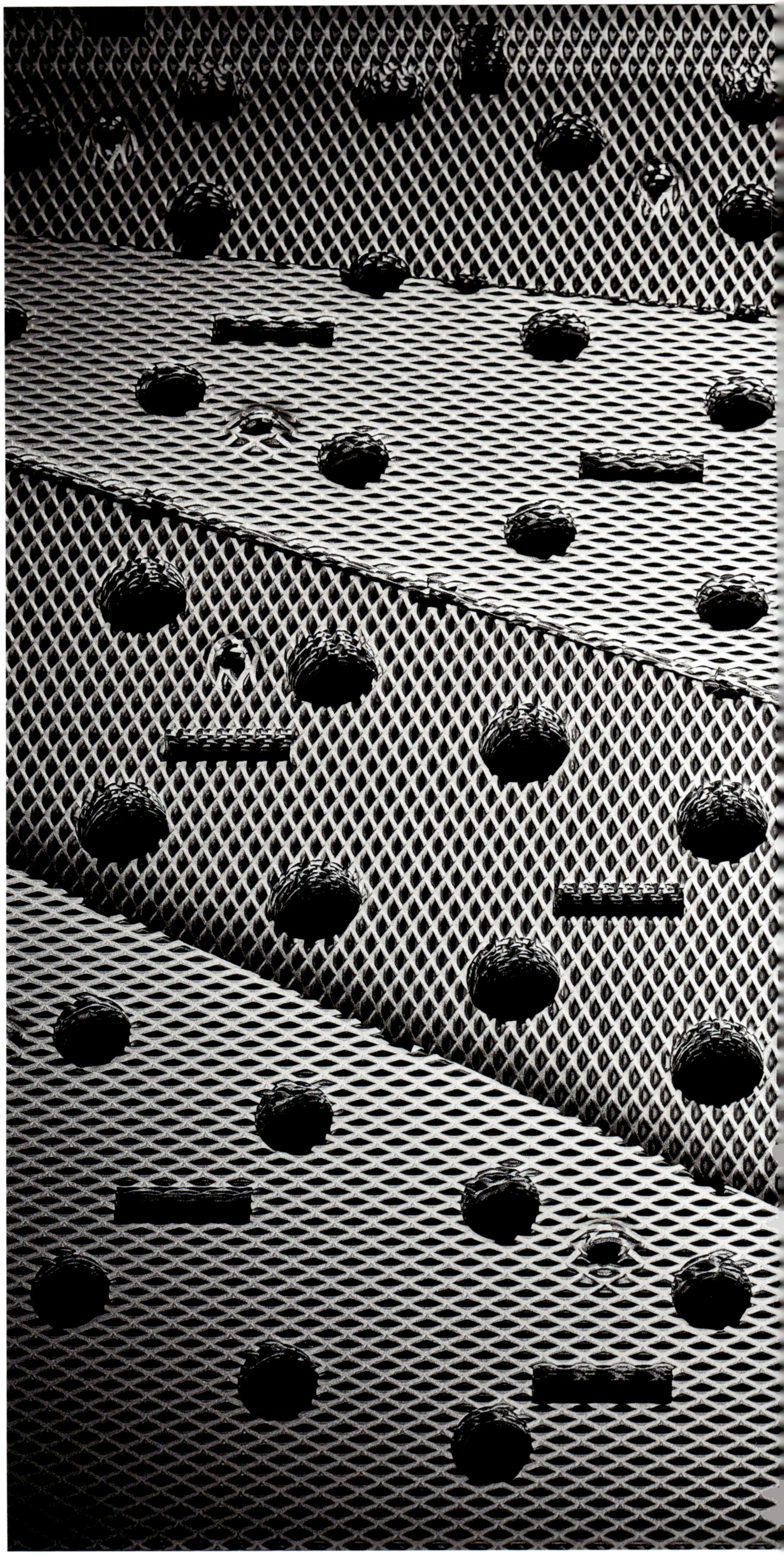

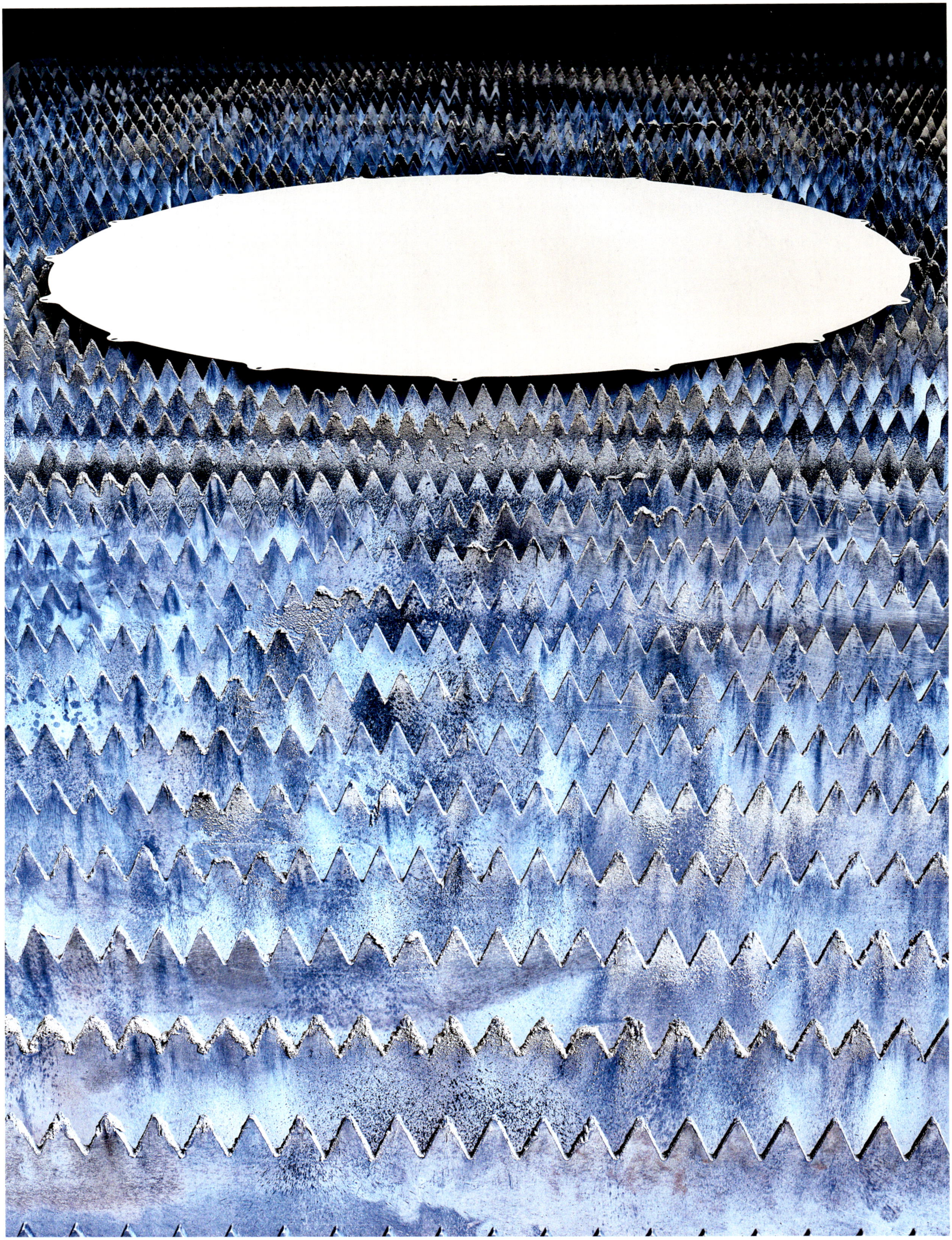

De Nora

Stories from a century of life

Texts by
Luca Masia

Photos by
Luca Campigotto

SKIRA

Cover
DSA® anode with chlor-alkali membrane technology

Page 1
Laboratory test cell
Milan

Pages 2-3
Electrodes for electroplating

Page 4
Electrodes for electrochlorination

Page 5
Titanium nozzles

Pages 6-7
Detail of an ozone generator

Page 8
Bipolar plate

Art Director
Luigi Fiore

Editorial Coordination
Vincenza Russo

Editing
Emanuela Chiesa

Layout
Evelina Laviano

Translations
Elizabeth Burke and Michael Carlos for NTL Firenze

Iconographical Research
Paola Achilli
Barbara Visentin

First published in Italy in 2023 by
Skira editore S.p.A.
Palazzo Casati Stampa
via Torino 61
20123 Milano
Italy
www.skira.net

Photo credits
All photographs are by Luca Campigotto with the exception of:
Photo Archivio De Nora: pp. 20, 22, 23, 26, 27, 36, 38, 39, 40, 41, 42, 43, 60, 62, 63, 64, 65, 67, 76, 77 top, 78, 80 top, 81, 90, 91, 95, 118, 119 right, 120, 121, 122, 123, 154, 155, 156, 157, 179
Photo Archivio De Nora - Credits Federico De Nora: pp. 24, 25, 116, 119 left
Photo Archivio De Nora – credits Fotocronache OLYMPIA: p. 66
Photo Archivio De Nora – credits Claudio Gallone©: pp. 79, 80 bottom
Photo Archivio De Nora – credits Lilithphoto, Daniele Lazzaretto and Emanuela Testa: pp. 94, 96, 97, 138, 140, 141, 143, 144, 166, 168, 169
Photo Archivio De Nora – Shutterstock: p. 152
Mondadori Portfolio/mauritius images / Novarc Images: p. 77 bottom
Archivio De Nora - Work by Anna Ramunni: pp. 174-175
Archivio De Nora - Work by Stefano Pietramala: pp. 180-181

Printed and bound in Italy. First edition

ISBN: 978-88-572-4922-3

Distributed in USA, Canada, Central & South America by
ARTBOOK | D.A.P. 75 Broad Street Suite 630, New York, NY 10004, USA.
Distributed elsewhere in the world by Thames and Hudson Ltd., 181A High Holborn, London WC1V 7QX, United Kingdom.

DE NORA

Contents in Augmented Reality (AR)
This volume is enhanced by Augmented Reality (AR) contents that enable readers to see the digital contents related to the different topics.

1. Download the Skira application from your App store
2. Select the Scan tool and point your smartphone on the images that have this icon

Celebrating one hundred years anniversary of a company is undoubtedly an important milestone, but doing so with the spirit and energy of this era is something unique. There is a near-perfect balance between experience and the desire to always get back into the game, and this gives us strength, positioning us for another phase of growth and success.

The De Nora company has a huge number of stories about the people who have contributed to the values and uniqueness of this incredible organization.
The most iconic representatives were those who ran the business, my grandfather Oronzio and my father Niccolò, who developed the business with perseverance, foresight and passion.

My brother and I, as the third generation, have picked up the baton, taking the group into a new era, maintaining the "historical" values, while incorporating modernity and restoring that drive towards the future that has always distinguished successful businesses.

This book is a way to express our thanks to all those who have worked and are working with us, by trying to explain what we are in words and images, and also to those who don't know us.
Nine chapters, nine stories. Each one is a story in itself, but they are all joined by a thread that starts in that distant month of August 1923 to arrive in present day.

Happy reading and I hope you enjoy it.

Federico De Nora

Contents

DSA® anode chlor-alkali
membrane technology

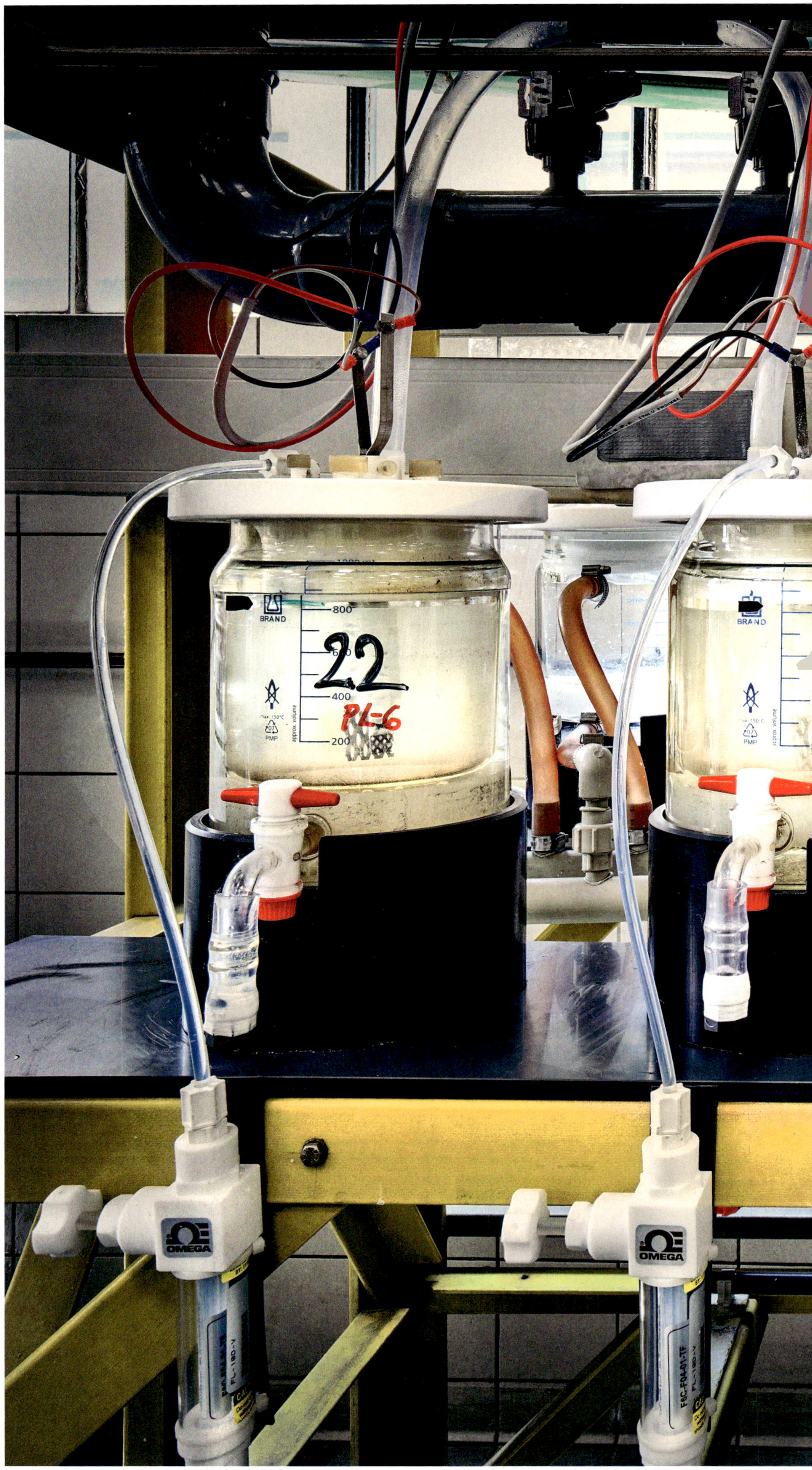

Laboratory test cells
Milan

9
PL-4
8
PL-3
OMEGA
OMEGA

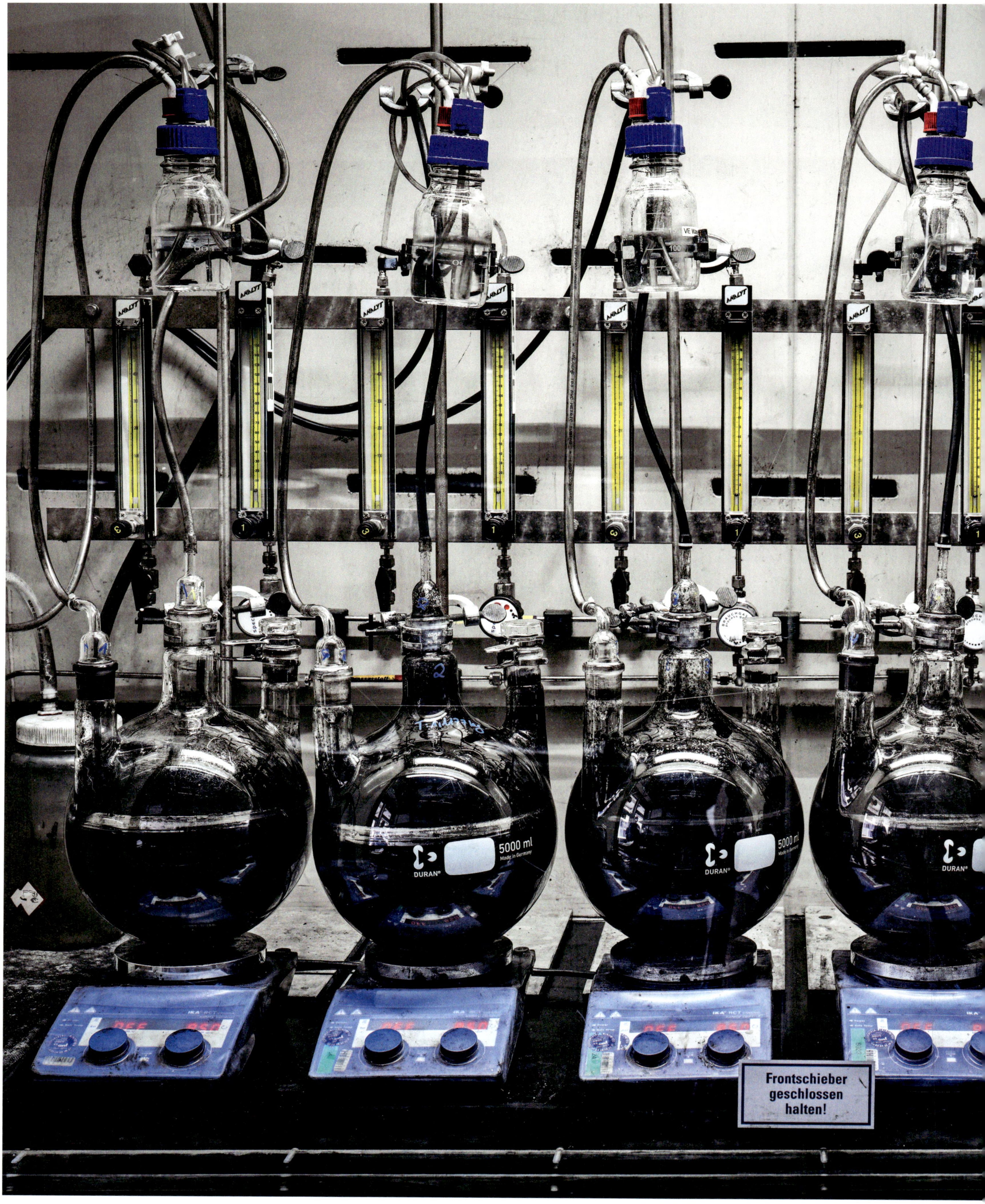
5000 ml
DURAN
Frontschieber
geschlossen
halten!

Laboratory reactors

Electrochemical magic

Fine dust hovers in the air. Particles of dust caressed by a beam of light in the still air of the laboratory. Light is matter. It filters through the window glass and traces the outline of a wooden workbench perpendicular to the radiator that is turned off, cold even in winter.
Each morning the light is the first to arrive in the laboratory. Shortly after, the door opens and in walks a young man. He takes off his jacket and puts on his lab coat, buttoning it as he goes over to the light-filled workbench. The air moves slightly at that point, and particles seem to dance against the light.
The electrochemistry laboratory at the University of Milan resembles a factory: the high ceiling, the huge south-facing windows. The light makes everything stand out, defining the workspaces.
The young researcher's name is Oronzio De Nora; he was born in Altamura in the late nineteenth century and is just over twenty years old. Having just graduated in industrial engineering, he's taking a specialization course in electrochemistry, working on chlor-alkali electrolysis. We see him open a drawer and take out a notebook, then take a pencil out of his lab coat pocket and start to write. In front of him, neatly lined up on the counter, are sealed glass containers and chemical compounds.
Oronzio is making a new electrolytic cell to produce sodium hypochlorite. The traditional laboratory cells consisted of a pair of electrodes immersed in a tank of salt water. The electrodes were arranged vertically or horizontally; Oronzio had the insight to tilt them in order to optimize the production process. He imagined the dense caustic soda sliding downwards, the chlorine gas rising upwards and the tilted electrode governing the reaction like a riverbank. The experimental model worked well and Oronzio De Nora has secured an industrial patent, the first of a long series.
Now, as he's jotting something down in his notebook, the light bounces off the white fabric of his lab coat. It grazes the surface of his hair. Everything else is in shadow; he stays focused on the problem at hand. Questions in search of answers. The pencil marks are just the tails of thoughts, the things that emerge from the inner tangle. A researcher's life is made up of questions, and answers that generate new questions. The failed experiment is never a defeat, only the beginning of a new line of research.

Oronzio De Nora had begun questioning things right from childhood. His father, Michele, had taught him to do this as they walked together in the Altamura countryside or in town under the cathedral's rose window. What a sight that Gothic cathedral's rose window was, when the light filtered in from above during mass and lit up the pews in the main aisle! Oronzio was always distracted by the restless movement of the dust grains which seemed to stir at the priest's words. His mother would nudge him with her elbow, give him a stern

▷

1920's, Milan Polytechnic, Chemical and Electrochemical Laboratory

1932, design for De Nora electrolytic cell

1932, De Nora electrolyzer for direct production of sodium hypochlorite

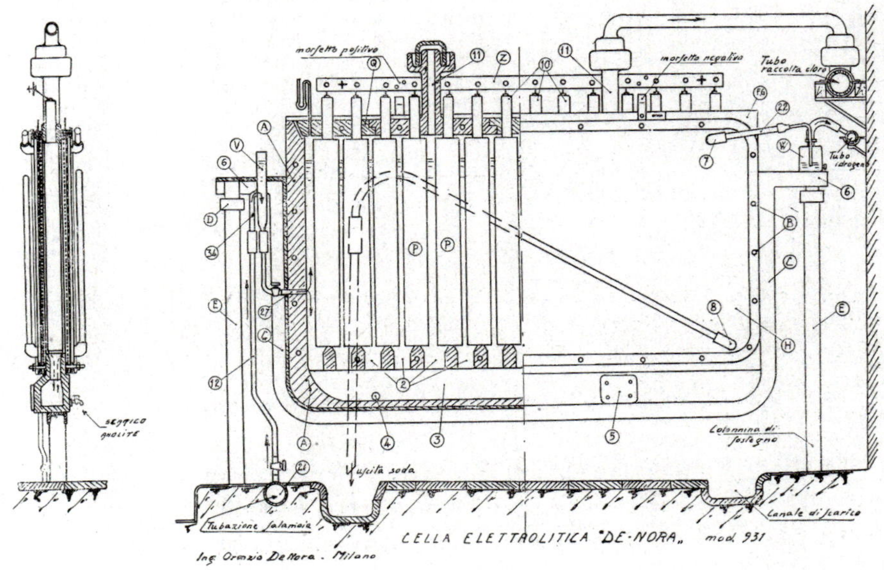

Fig. 3.

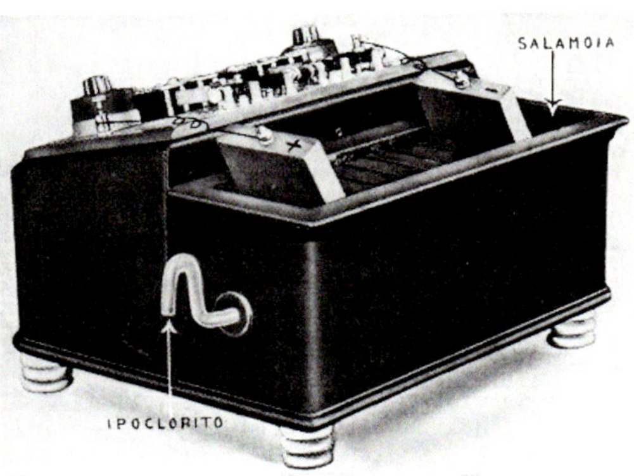

look, and point to the pulpit. His father, on the other hand, would lean towards him and whisper in his ear: "Atmospheric dust mixed with a pinch of cosmic dust, billions of years old!"

Oronzio's father would pick a stone up off the ground, show it to his son, and tell him about nature's perfection; he would point out the infinite planes of perspective enclosed in a fragment of rock formed over time. The white lines are the stone's scars, he would tell him, where calcite has settled filling the fractures in the stone. Nothing ever happened by chance in his father's talks. He was an engineer, in charge of the Apulian aqueduct that collected water and irrigated the fields of the Murge, which grew the wheat for the city's bakeries. On leaving mass, the aroma of bread from the Santa Chiara bakery already promised a feast. Bread that was still warm, wrapped in crinkly paper. Oronzio would tear off a piece with his fingers and feel the dark, crunchy crust and firm dough inside. His father would take a piece too and walk home telling him about leavening, sourdough, the bacterial microflora in the dough of flour and water coming into contact with the air and the environment.

"Dust as well?" asked Oronzio.

"Atmospheric dust, for sure! And who knows, maybe a pinch of cosmic dust."

Oronzio remembered all those talks, when physics and chemistry became part of everyday life. The days of the first questions. He had only been ten years old when he wondered how to light the nativity scene. It was the beginning of the twentieth century and there was no electricity in Altamura. His father showed him a diagram of a dichromate battery and Oronzio made one using coal from their chimney and zinc sheeting from construction sites. How satisfying it was to light up that nativity scene on Christmas Eve of 1909! Better than the rose window in the cathedral!

In the laboratory of the University of Milan, Oronzio De Nora is perfecting the prototype of his electrolytic cell with inclined electrodes. The morning sun is now high. Earlier, the light seemed like a dense, compact fluid that only illuminated what it touched, but now it's spread through the room like a gas. It's everywhere.

As he works, Oronzio cuts his finger with a splinter of glass. Unsure of how to disinfect the wound, he instinctively dips his

Cathedral of Altamura, Bari, Italy

1925, Milan Trade Fair, Oronzio De Nora at the entrance to his booth

finger into the brine of the electrolytic cell, just as he did as a child at the seaside: to heal the cuts he got on the rocks, he would bathe them in seawater. He leaves his finger in the cell water, daydreaming about the magical powers of that salt water traversed by streams of electricity. Then he dries it carefully, wraps a handkerchief around the wound and gets back to work.

When he removes the bandage, the wound is healed.

New questions leap into the researcher's mind. Was it actually chlorinated and electrified water that disinfected the cut and accelerated the healing? Once again, Oronzio De Nora relies on his father. He takes off his lab coat, puts on his jacket and closes the lab door behind him. He leaves the university and heads for the post office. Every evening, Oronzio regularly writes an account of the day's events on a postcard that he sends to his father. But when he wants to send him something bigger, he goes to the Central Station and puts the parcel in the overhead compartment of the night train to Bari. They've agreed on a carriage and a seat, so the next morning his father waits for the train to arrive at the station, climbs into the carriage and picks up the parcel.

After reading his son's last postcard, Michele De Nora immediately asks him for a sample of the prodigious find. Oronzio fills a small bottle from the laboratory, carefully seals it and sends it off. From that day forward, father and son launch into an intense exchange. More wounds and more healings follow. The scientific experiment is repeated.

Oronzio and Michele try diluting the product in various proportions and realize that it has a vast range of possible applications, from treating wounds to washing fruit and vegetables and disinfecting water.

They analyze all the variables and formulate their first hypotheses. Oronzio is convinced that the sodium hypochlorite generated by the electrolytic reaction is capable of releasing a kind of active oxygen that then combines with organic compounds in the wound. Oronzio calls it "electrolytic oxychloride". Not exactly a catchy name for a product that would go on to become a commercial success. His father suggests they think of it in Greek, think of the term *muche*, wound. And then maybe add the alpha privative, common even in current Italian.

And so Amuchina was born. A stroke of luck, a touch of genius.

A few months after Amuchina was invented, Count Piovene came to the offices of the Milan Polytechnic to meet Professor Carraro. The aristocrat from Vicenza, father of the writer and journalist Guido Piovene—who in 1923 was little more than a boy—owned a factory in Milan that produced sodium hypochlorite. The design of his electrolytic cells was an old one and he wanted to make the plant more efficient. Carraro immediately referred him to Oronzio De Nora, his brightest student. He took him to the laboratory and introduced him to the young researcher. While the count was explaining the problem, Oronzio carried on working on the cell with the inclined electrodes. He listened with the mind of an engineer, but he had the hands of a mechanic. Oronzio knew how to turn ideas into reality. He had the rare talent of being able to make things work. He was a tenacious innovator, always willing to question the certainties of the past, ready to explore new territories. In the end, the aristocratic industrialist and the young electrochemist shook hands. Oronzio took off his lab coat, put on his overcoat and closed the laboratory door behind him. He made his way through the university, after which the count guided him towards Martesana, where the plant was located.

The plant was relatively small: eighteen cells needed to be updated. Oronzio, however, was alone. The count asked him what he needed to do the job.

"Nothing."

Michele De Nora, father of Oronzio

First sign of the De Nora plant in Milan

"An advance on expenses?"
"Nothing."
"Materials, equipment?"
"Nothing."
The Count was embarrassed.
"When could you start?"
"Now. But I'd need a lab coat. I left mine at the university."
It took two days of uninterrupted work to upgrade Count Piovene's cells. When he'd finished, he took off the lab coat that didn't belong to him. He'd also asked for a notebook that he'd filled with observations. He carefully avoided returning it, putting it in his jacket pocket instead. During the course of his work, he'd come up with some valuable ideas: interesting questions to ponder. When it was time to get paid, Oronzio shook the count's hand.
"It was a pleasure."
Piovene looked him straight in the eye and held the strong hand of the young man who seemed to live outside of this world.
"I'll tell you what: now that we've met, I'll put you in charge of building eighteen new electrolytic cells. You take care of everything. Design, construction, assembly, service. I paid two thousand liras each for the old cells. Please determine the cost of the new ones."
We have to imagine those two men with their minds focused on the future and the rest of their bodies anchored in the past. A difficult thing to explain. Almost impossible to understand nowadays. We can try, though. We can stop and take in the expressions on their faces, the firm handshake, the tone of Oronzio De Nora's voice when he said:
"One thousand five hundred liras each."
The count immediately advanced him a third of the sum. Oronzio, who had never had money in his pocket, suddenly found himself with nine thousand liras in his wallet. He left the university and bought a new lab coat. He then looked for a space in which to set up a mechanical workshop. He found a place near the Central Station and the Pirelli factory. At the back was a wooden shack. He salvaged a workbench from a junkyard, bought the materials and hired a worker. Then he started building the new cells for Count Piovene. The future of the De Nora company had already begun.

In the years to follow, Oronzio invented an entirely new cell with vertical percolation electrodes. In 1927, he produced seventy of these new cells and began exporting the first units abroad, particularly to Eastern Europe. The work increased. Industry needed electrochemistry. For Superpila in Florence, Oronzio had to build a plant to produce manganese dioxide. For the occasion, he invented a filtration system inspired by the way that Altamura farmers crushed their olives: he used woolen fabrics that were resistant to acid, squeezing them with a system of rotating levers and filtering the liquid through a thick sackcloth gauze.

By the beginning of the 1930s, the De Nora company had already produced more than a hundred units in its new premises on Via

Oronzio De Nora with his wife Linda Taglialatela

Arquà. This production facility had been purpose-built to meet the demands of the market. By the mid-twentieth century, chlorine and caustic soda were already essential to a large part of industrial production. After the war, they became the index by which to measure a country's level of industrialization. There was a world to conquer and Oronzio was no longer alone. His brother Vittorio, who was thirteen years his junior, joined him from Altamura; he was another chemistry genius. Having graduated with the highest honors, in 1934, he was the youngest Italian engineer. He had then taken specialization courses abroad and been involved in scientific research. Finally, he had been appointed assistant professor at the Milan Polytechnic. This training in the sciences brought Oronzio and Vittorio De Nora together. But there was more: the two brothers complemented each other, and together they formed a team that was as solid as a family. They had sharp minds, efficient practicality, and a talent for sales. The factory on Via Arquà had survived the Second World War bombings and was now used as a warehouse. The company moved to the new building on Via Bistolfi, in the Lambrate area of the Ortica district. This was the site of the sales offices, research laboratory, and design department. Oronzio also had a space for a vegetable garden, which he tended personally with that somewhat maniacal attention to detail that he was known for. Sometimes he would stay behind in the evening and walk through the furrows of soil, hand in hand with his wife, who he still treated as his cherished fiancée. He had mastered the art of staying young. The vegetable garden at the center of the company also took on a symbolic value. It consolidated the bond with the land, defining a serene environment where the perfection of nature is perceived as being at one with human toil. In the humble clods of soil in that land that had been wrested from the concrete city, Oronzio witnessed the passing of the seasons, the tenacious repetition of daily miracles. The garden

1928, De Nora installation in the Rossari & Varzi plant in Galliate, Novara, Italy

embodies everything: chemistry, physics, biology, philosophy, art. The mystery of life. At every moment of the day, the vegetable garden on Via Bistolfi reminded him that in order to grow big, you have to stay small. To think and act like an artisan, even when you become an industrialist.

Oronzio and Vittorio De Nora realized that although the electrolytic process behind the production of chlorine and caustic soda was simple, it could be improved. After inspecting a plant in Lodi where frequent accidents were occurring, Oronzio designed a new cell with a vertical decomposer that allowed reagents to circulate against the current and that could also be inspected from below. The prototype was installed in Tolmezzo, in the Pirelli group's paper mill. Shortly afterwards, he focused on the materials for constructing the cells and perfected a design using polished granite instead of concrete for the flow of mercury. He also used a very light and flexible vulcanized rubber cover, which made it possible to adjust the position of the electrodes.

De Nora's new mercury cell was installed in Argentina in 1949; soon afterwards the brothers from Altamura built a plant for the U.S. Army, at that time deployed in the Korean War.

Over the next twenty years, the De Nora mercury cells spread around the world. Forty per cent of the world's chlorine and caustic soda would be produced with De Nora electrolyzers, which were increasingly powerful, reliable and efficient. It had started with the small paper mill in Tolmezzo and extended to large-scale sites in Japan, the United States and the Soviet Union. Throughout the world, all production processes were accelerating dramatically. Where there was industry, there was chlor-alkali, and where there was chlor-alkali, there was De Nora. It had spread from the Altamura countryside to the rest of the world, passing through Via Bistolfi, where there was always a vegetable garden to tend. A place where one could grow old in peace and take an evening stroll with a wife who would forever be the cherished fiancée.

Detail of a laser welding
device

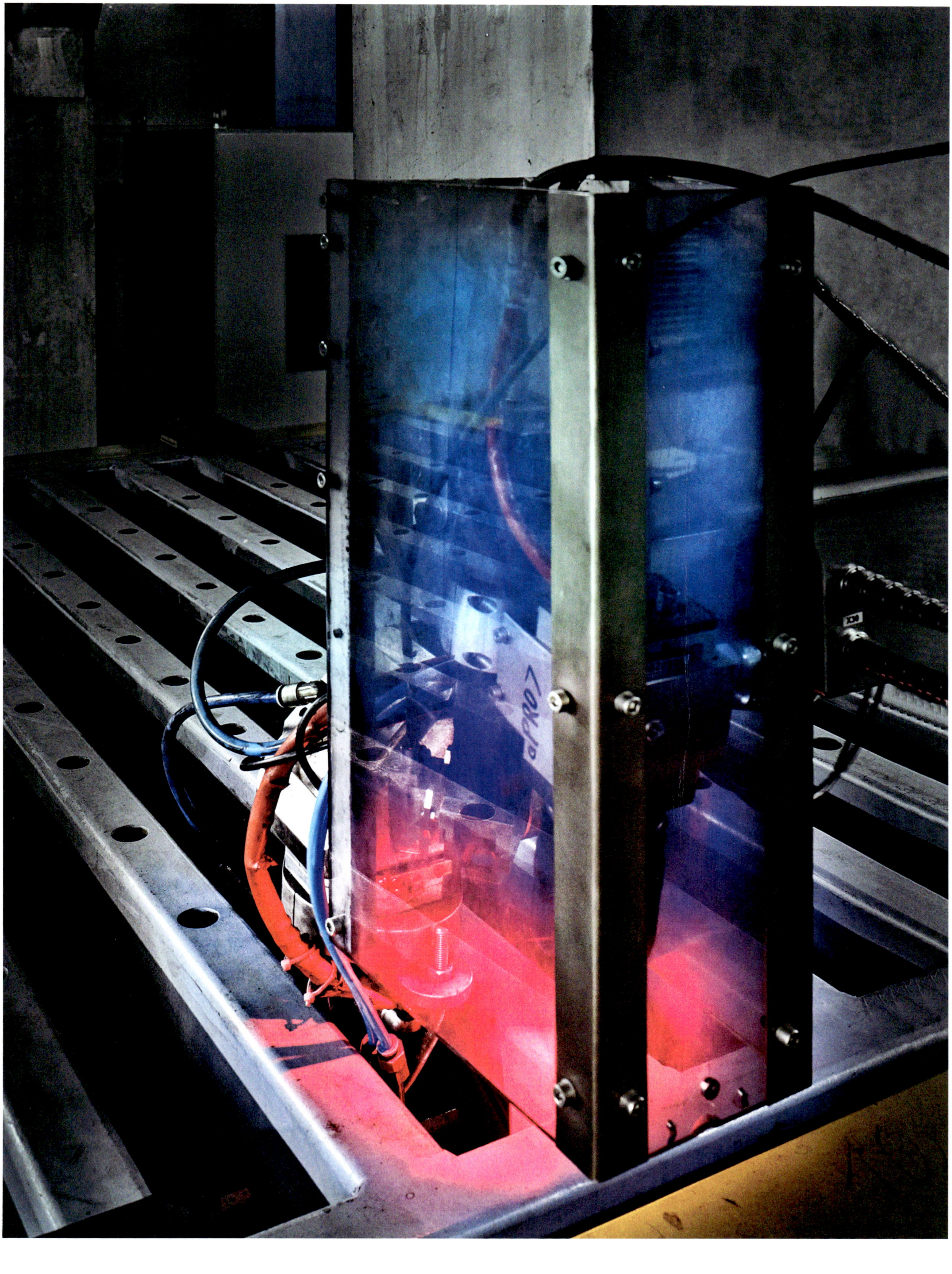

DSA® anode chlor-alkali
membrane technology

SALAMOIA
SALAMOIA

Laboratory test cells,Milan

Laboratory test cells
Milan

A splash of paint

Fear in the night, on the stormy sea. The water washes over the deck of the fishing boat and the young man is almost swallowed up by the bloated oilskin. His feet are freezing inside his boots, his hands are sliced up by the fishing line, and his fingers are stiff with cold. The sea terrified him even as a child, when he used to listen to his grandfather's and father's stories. Then he embarked and the sea became his home. Out there on the water, during the fishing season, time passes slowly. But it ages you quickly.

There are nights when only the boat knows what to do. When it's the only thing that knows how to talk to the waves. Mountains of seawater. The hull holds fast, brings the men home. And every time the night and the sea bite into his soul, the young fisherman swears he won't go back. But then he disembarks and forgets his promise. He's a sailor.

On land he shakes the captain's hand, pockets his pay and takes refuge in the harbor bar. There are three things he has to do. The second is a cold beer, the third a hot shower. The first and most important thing is the one he does last. He waits for night to fall then goes back to the boat. In silence, he stares for a long time at the dark paint on the hull. It's like a prayer.

When you're at sea, you're nothing, and a good boat can be everything. The young man knows this and wants to exalt it. So, when he's absolutely sure that nobody can see him, he climbs aboard. He goes to the bow and leans out over the broadside. He stays like that for a while, as though hovering over the water, clinging to the air. Then he lets one arm dangle and strokes the hull with his fingers. A kind of caress.

In that very moment, in Milan, in Via Bistolfi, Oronzio De Nora is writing a letter to his brother, who is in the United States, in Pennsville, Ohio. The De Nora family is building a large chlorine and caustic soda plant for Diamond Shamrock, an American chemical giant. In the 1950s, their mercury cells reached very high levels of efficiency and became a global benchmark. But the research continues. The innovations conceived by Oronzio, Vittorio and their team of researchers are affecting all the essential parameters that govern electrochemical reactions: energy consumption, reaction speed, purity of the materials produced, and operating costs. More specifically, already in the Diamond Shamrock plant, cells with a bottom that can withstand ever-increasing electrical loads, a graphite-filled vertical decomposer for better mercury recirculation, with the introduction of special anodes to reduce energy losses, are installed.

The ink flows smoothly from the nib to the paper and draws out a stream of words. Ideas bounce around in Oronzio's mind. He's particularly obsessed with how fragile the graphite electrodes are. For some years now, he's been dreaming of creating a new metal component that is efficient,

▷

1960s, Oronzio De Nora celebrates with staff in the cafeteria of the Milan plant on the Via Bistolfi

1960s, De Nora research laboratory

resistant and doesn't deteriorate. The collaboration with Diamond Shamrock is also about this joint research, the romantic idea of joining forces to achieve common goals. Two brothers, an ocean apart. They use the telephone to talk about things, and pen and paper to explain them.
The most promising material would appear to be titanium. The problem is corrosion, which makes it inert to the point of impeding the current's flow. Oronzio had devised a special platinum film to combine the strength of titanium with the conductivity of platinum. He'd had excellent results, but the costs were excessive. They needed to find something new. They needed to look to nature's perfection to find the simple solution to a complex problem.
In his letters, Oronzio meticulously describes the technical details of the experiments to his brother, making notes on the new questions lurking within the first questions, partial answers. In this last letter, he adds that something new seems to be happening up north, along the cold windy shores of Holland, from Rotterdam to Amsterdam. Amphibious places laced with canals embedded in the land. It seems that a researcher—a certain Henri Beer—has detected a simple material that enables a good electrochemical reaction when applied to titanium. Oronzio ends his letter by saying, "We should meet this researcher. It seems that he has a brother and I'd like to see his studies. I may have a few questions for him."

It's not hard to imagine Vittorio De Nora re-reading his brother's letter several times to make sure he hasn't missed anything. Then he puts it back into the envelope and a shiver of excitement goes up his spine. Finally, we see him boarding an intercontinental flight to Italy. He and Oronzio then take the train to Schiedam, a small village between Rotterdam and The Hague, near Delft, the landscape of Vermeer.
Dr. Beer does in fact have a brother. But he's a writer, a mystery author. He's not the one behind the electrochemical research lab that is experimenting—subject to all the limitations of the case—with a brown coating that, when applied to titanium, allows strong electrical currents to pass through it and seems impervious to corrosion. Henri Beer is a tall, thin man with a broad forehead and thinning hair combed carefully back. His glasses follow the line of his eyelids, and he has bags under his eyes. His prominent nose pokes out between the

lenses like the keel of a hull, the deep furrows in his cheeks drag his mouth down. His upper lip is another straight line, the more pronounced lower lip gives him a vaguely sad but intelligent expression. He speaks softly, smiling often. He explains that it's ruthenium, the least noble of platinum group metals. He's coated the titanium with a thin layer of ruthenium.

Oronzio listens carefully, but he's puzzled. Ruthenium isn't supposed to be particularly effective in electrolytic reactions. There must be something else. The only thing to do is to keep asking.

To give a rough idea of the answers, Dr. Beer invites the De Nora brothers to walk along the shore with him. It's a cool afternoon, with a wan light. The three researchers walk around the docks and discuss their world, far from the rest of the world. Something researchers often do and they manage it rather well. Henri Beer points to a fishing boat just back from a trip out. He explains that those boats spend their lives at sea, and yet the shipwrights know what kind of paint to use on their hulls so that they're resistant to corrosion. Who knows, maybe they've been mixing these paints since the time of the Vikings, and today they use these magic potions to paint their boats, the fishermen's homes that bring them back to land after the storms.

The north can suddenly become a dark, cold landscape. They decide to continue

First DSA® anodes installed in a Diamond Shamrock plant, USA

DSA® anode chlor-alkali mercury technology

their discussion in the harbor bar, which is full of fishermen. There's a young man there too having a beer with a vivacious girl a few tables away. Henri Beer loves beer. It's in his name. He orders two mugs of unfiltered dark double malt, something for connoisseurs. Vittorio prefers wine, but he's curious. Oronzio doesn't drink and keeps asking questions.

Wiping the foam from his thin lips, Dr. Beer explains that the coating he's made and wants to patent is a mixture of ruthenium and the resin that is applied to the hulls of fishing boats. He also explains that before using the coating, he subjects the mixture to a special heat treatment in the presence of air. All very empirical, as it often is with innovations. Who knows? Perhaps at that moment Who knows, perhaps at that moment Oronzio De Nora will have remembered that cut that miraculously healed by dipping his finger into the brine of his first electrolytic cell. Amuchina had also been invented by accident—an intuitive hunch. But then only by rigorously studying the phenomenon were they able to understand and reproduce it. Scientific analysis as the art of questioning. Asking the right questions, of course. The only ones that can keep the research alive.

On the return trip to Milan, Oronzio is already making notes. During the reaction between the ruthenium and the resin of the fishing boats, a specific substance must form, which probably changes during the heat treatment. The first thing to do is thoroughly analyze the resin samples from the hulls, using the most cutting-edge technology available.

In the months that followed, the lab analyses confirmed Oronzio and Vittorio's hunch. During heat treatment, the ruthenium resin decomposed to form ruthenium dioxide, which proved to be an excellent catalyst for electrochemical reactions. The path ahead was clear. In the late 1960s, the research team led by Oronzio and Vittorio De Nora discovered that it was possible to create a paint containing both

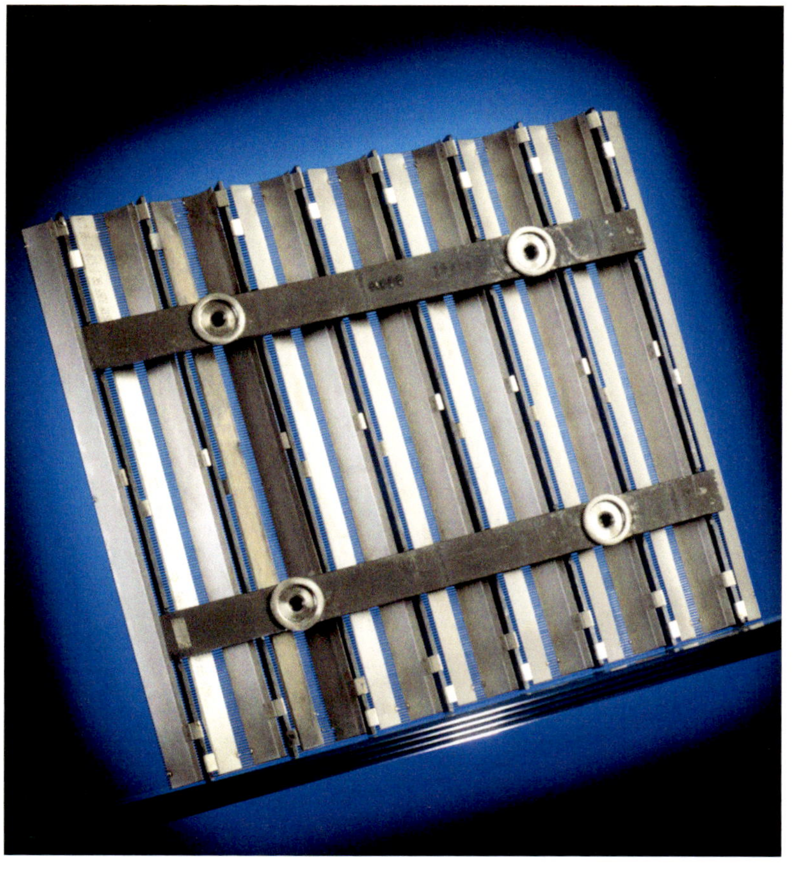

1960s, workshop worker at the De Nora plant in Milan

ruthenium dioxide and titanium dioxide. The latter made the paint compatible with the electrode base, capable of anchoring stably to the metal. On the other hand, ruthenium dioxide enabled the electrochemical reactions that Beer had already seen in his work.

It was an exciting time: an endless series of experiments and analysis were carried out to scientifically validate the hunches and imaginative intuitions. Oronzio cultivated creativity in the conviction that scientific knowledge was everyone's heritage, but that only imagination allowed us to see new horizons, to provide glimpses of the future. Working beside him meant sharing the fatigue of labor and intense feelings. Under his direction, the team became a unified group and everything was managed together. Even the failures, which were never defeats.

"Without mistakes, nothing is discovered," he often repeated to his colleagues. Research, like life, is a never-ending game to be played one move at a time. A precious collection of moments. In technical meetings he paid close attention to everyone equally, university professors and lab technicians. Once, a drawing of the cloister of San Paolo fuori le Mura in Rome in the notes of a recently hired young researcher caught Oronzio's eye, a hasty sketch on a paper napkin, but full of details and perfect proportions, despite the fast drawing. Oronzio noticed that drawing and gave the young man an important assignment.

"Why?" The researcher asked him, knowing that he didn't have the experience required.

"I've seen your drawings," Oronzio replied. "You don't look, you observe. You'll do a good job."

Oronzio was fascinated by people's eyes. He watched them carefully when he listened to them speak. He often said that words were only a part of speech, it was the eyes that said the rest.

He didn't know any languages, only a bit of German and French. But in meetings he understood foreigners by looking at them. And when he listened to the translations, he would often shake his head, dissatisfied. "He didn't say that," he would exclaim to the translator. "I saw something else!"

Despite his success, Oronzio continued to straighten used nails and keep the packaging from the titanium sheets. He used them to wrap gifts. Nothing deserved to be thrown away. A bit like energy, which is neither created nor destroyed, but transformed. The best day of the week was Sunday, when he could work alone, just as he had done as a young man in those early mornings in the university lab. Almost fifty years had passed since then. Little more than a blink of an eye for Oronzio De Nora.

The brothers from Altamura patented the new titanium electrodes coated with mixed metal oxides, called them DSA® electrodes and prepared to sell them globally. Chlor-alkali was now everywhere: expanses of electrolytic cells—often made by De Nora—equipped with traditional, fragile graphite anodes. The new electrodes were set to revolutionize that landscape. But as we know, the world tends to resist innovation. Selling DSA® technology called for an idea that was just as brilliant as the resin of the North Sea fishing boats. The genius in the family for this kind of thing was Vittorio. Everyone called him the professor. Even the Americans at Diamond Shamrock, who were fascinated by his gentle ways, his calm tones, his natural tendency to always give the best of himself.

"We don't have to sell the DSA® electrodes," he told his brother, "just lease them."

Oronzio looked him in the eye to grasp the hidden meaning behind his words, but couldn't find any. He was quiet for what seemed like an infinity. His brother came to his rescue.

"We lease them for a certain period and base the price on the actual production of chlorine and caustic soda. If they don't work, they can return them. But because they do work..."

Vittorio De Nora, brother of Oronzio

1969, traditional Japanese ceremony for the opening of the Permelec-Chiba plant, Japan

A smile began to appear on Oronzio's lips. He never ceased to marvel at good ideas. The show of intelligence.
Vittorio packed his things and went abroad. He visited De Nora customers who had installed traditional graphite electrodes, then ventured out to explore new and still unknown markets. Japan, first of all. It only took him six months to forge new relationships and close a series of deals aimed at doubling domestic chlor-alkali production.

No Japanese person can resist admiring the spectacle of blossoming cherry trees. *Hanami* is the local term. Foreigners also celebrate the beauty of nature. A fragile, precious epiphany. Strolling along Fujisawa's tree-lined avenues, Oronzio couldn't help but think of the vegetable garden on Via Bistolfi, of the exact perfection of things a moment before they vanish. Like dreams, before waking. *Sakura* means the blossoming flower in Japanese: enclosed in its beauty is its end. The relentless reminder that nothing is forever.
In the spring of 1969, the De Nora brothers often traveled to Fujisawa, some fifty kilometers south of Tokyo. They were negotiating with the giant Mitsui, a company that dated far back to 1600, when Mitsui Takatoshi opened a kimono shop. It was now one of the most powerful and diversified industrial groups in Japan and the world.
That same year, Mitsui and De Nora founded a joint venture. The new company was called Permelec Electrode and it became the production center for DSA® technology in Asia. De Nora's new titanium electrodes, coated with mixed metal oxides, become the new global benchmark in the industry. They already had an aris-

322- A traditional Japanese ceremony purification plant or factory opening which was held at Permelec-Chiba Plant on October 1st,1969

1970s, Oronzio and Vittorio De Nora with a company manager

tocratic aura, like industrial jewels. They couldn't actually be owned, only leased. They blossomed like *sakura*, but never faded. When the coating wore off, they only had to be "repainted". All included, of course, in the lease contract.

Traditional graphite electrodes were simple components of electrolytic cells, and the De Nora DSA® technology became the heart of new chlor-alkali production plants. Often, in chemistry books, the evocative image of the chlor-alkali tree appears next to the diagram of an electrolytic cell. A solid trunk, an infinite number of branches and an immense canopy. In detergents, textile fibers, mechanics, plastics, glass and pharmaceuticals, chlorine and caustic soda make up the trunk on which the complexity of modern industrial society rests. The trunk of that tree is made up of electrolytic cells. And at the heart of each cell are De Nora electrodes.

PMX ® production at the De Nora plant in Cologno Monzese, Milan, Italy

page 46
Detail of an ozone generator

page 47
Electromagnetic component of an ozone generator (inductance)

Laboratory quality test
Cologno Monzese, Milan,
Italy

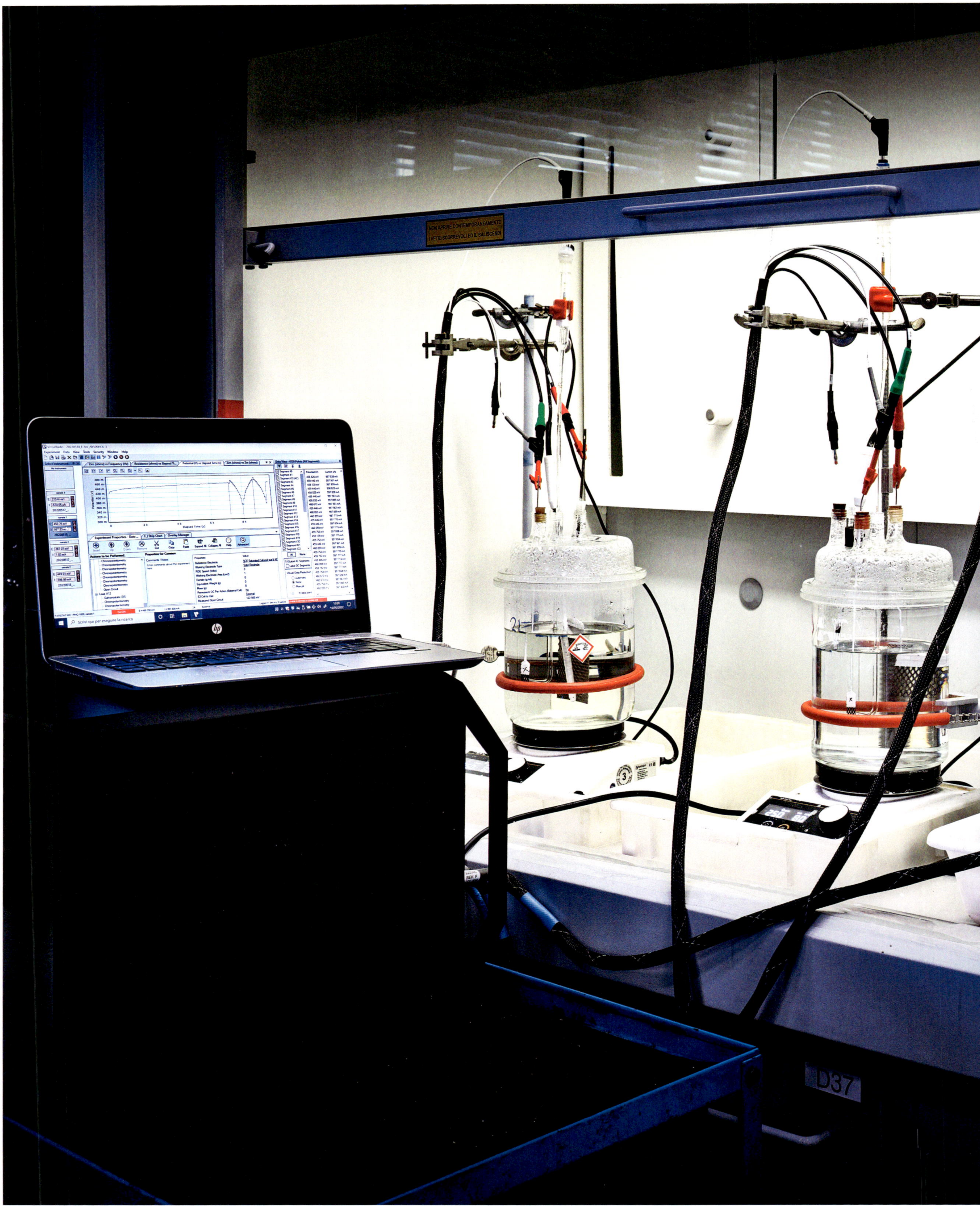
NON APRIRE CONTEMPORANEAMENTE
I VETRI SCORREVOLI ED IL SALISCENDI
D37

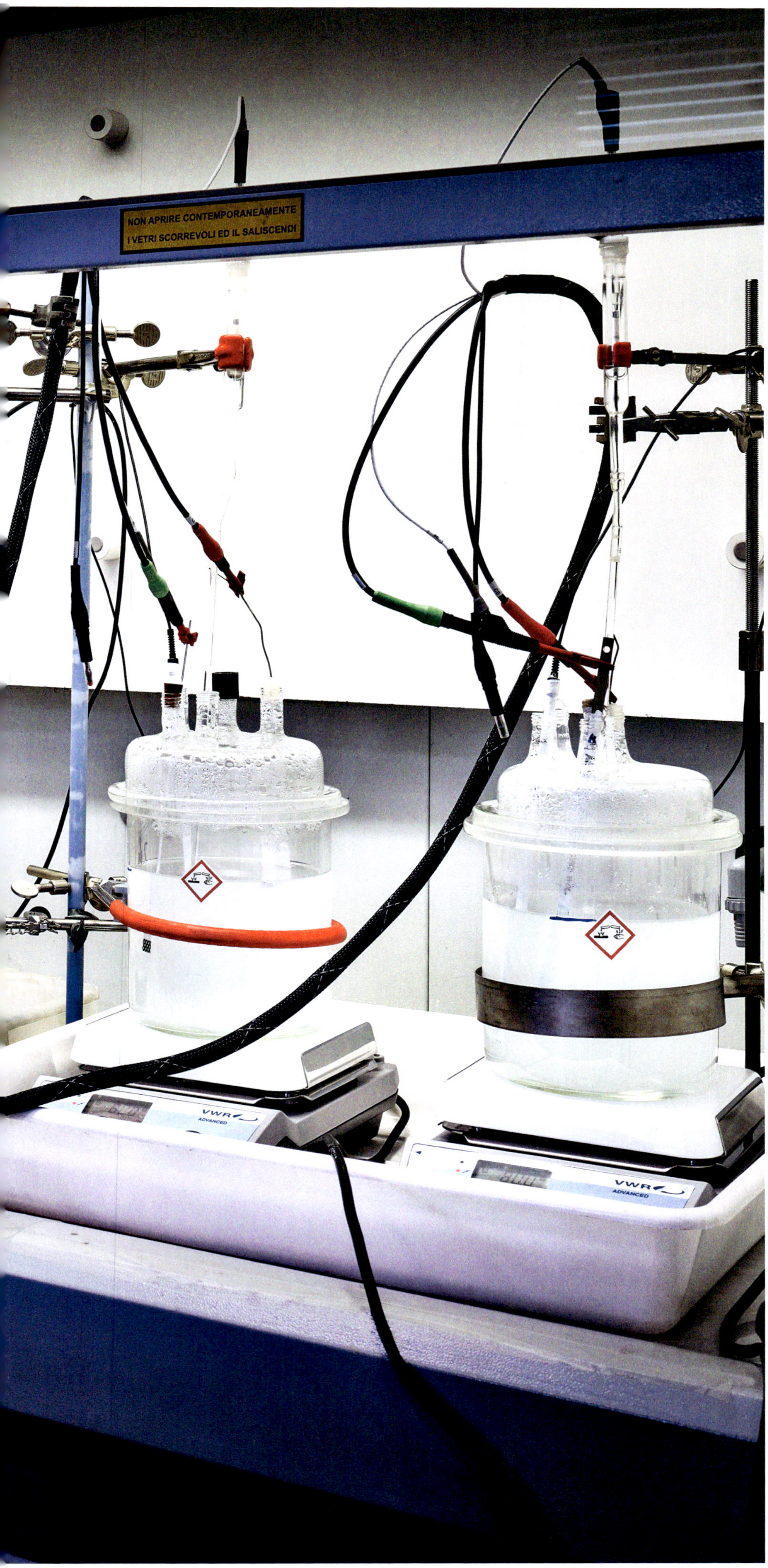

Analytics laboratory, Milan

Following pages
Laboratory test cells,
Milan

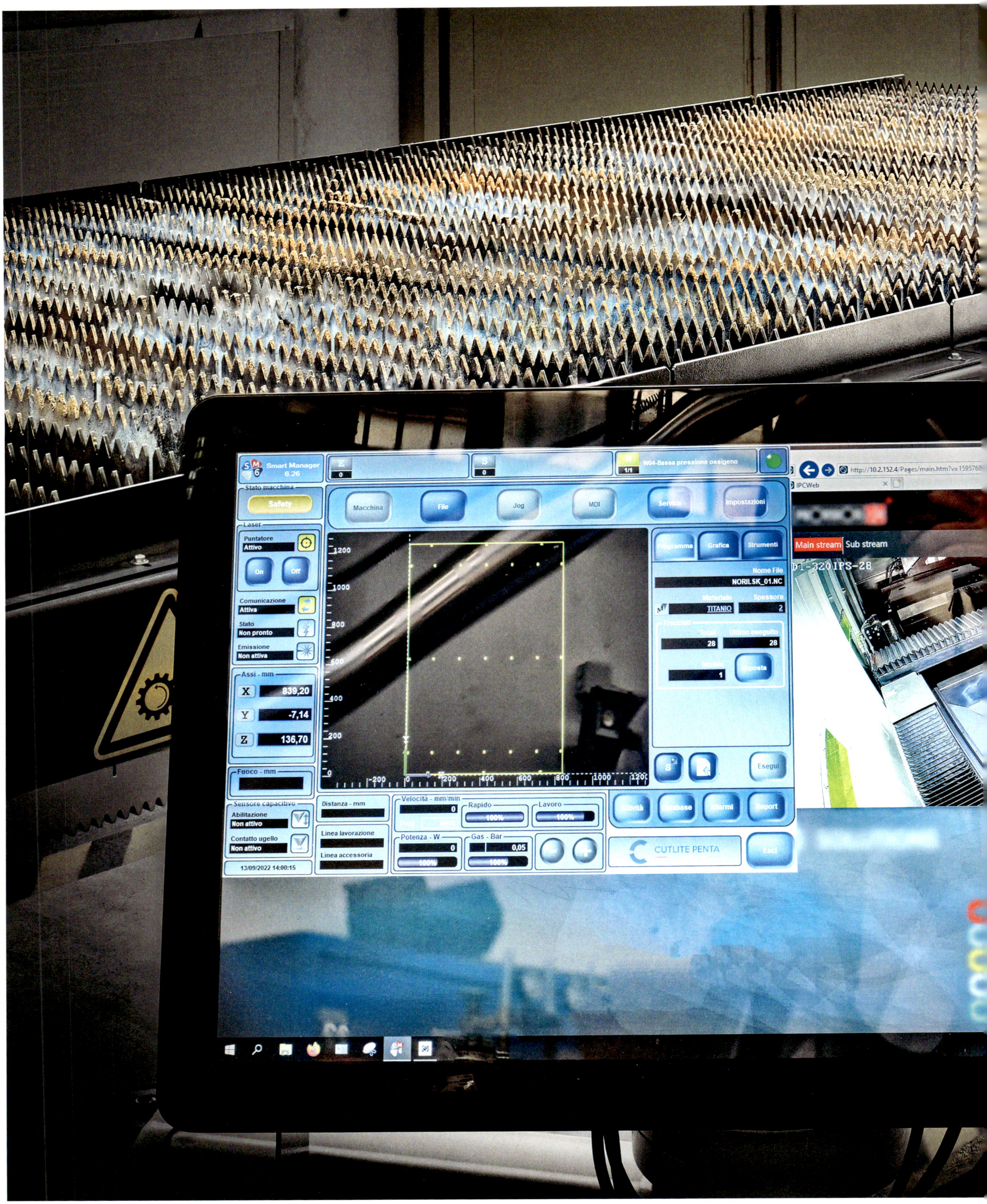

Smart Manager 6.26
W04-Bassa pressione ossigeno
Stato macchina
Safety
Macchina
File
Jog
MDI
Service
Impostazioni
Laser
Puntatore
Attivo
On
Off
Comunicazione
Attiva
Stato
Non pronto
Emissione
Non attiva
Assi - mm
X 839,20
Y -7,14
Z 136,70
Fuoco - mm
Sensore capacitivo
Abilitazione
Non attivo
Contatto ugello
Non attivo
13/09/2022 14:00:15
Distanza - mm
Linea lavorazione
Linea accessoria
Velocità - mm/min
Rapido
Lavoro
Potenza - W
Gas - Bar
0,05
Grafica
Strumenti
Nome File
NORILSK_01.NC
Materiale
Spessore
TITANIO
2
Esegui
CUTLITE PENTA
Esci
IPCWeb
Main stream
Sub stream

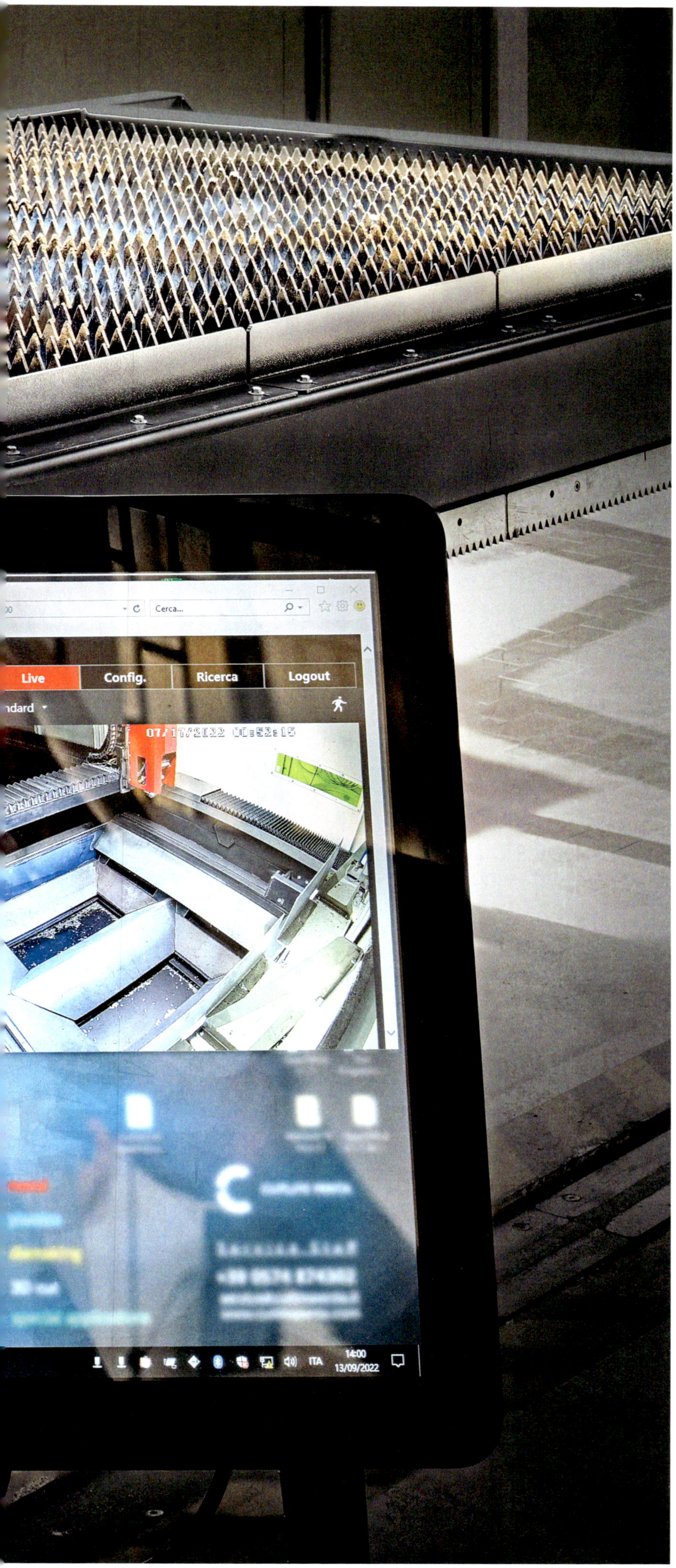

De Nora plant, quality control, Rodenbach

DSA® anode chlor-alkali
membrane technology

Detail of a Seaclor®
component

New horizons

The beginning of the piece is a time of waiting, a suspended interval. The brushes glide softly over the snare drum, in expectation of the piano's terse notes. They're like stars that slowly become bright at nightfall. And finally, the trumpet: it's Chet Baker's *Almost Blue*.

Niccolò De Nora keeps his eyes shut. He is imagining a railroad that crosses the country, passing through the broad landscape that stretches into the distance. A train moves ahead while he lies motionless on the tracks. The trumpet has the deep sound of a generous heart. Each beat is a breath, and each breath a rush of life. The music in his head takes him away, far from the world of humans.

He was kidnapped on 11 January 1977 in Piazza della Repubblica in Milan. He spent his captivity chained to a cot. He saved himself because he managed to do nothing, just to imagine.

In addition to music, he liked painting. Brush in hand, he took pains to imitate Mondrian—the shapes, the balanced spaces and light of the colors. Mondrian's paintings were like musical scores: you could read the music hidden in the architecture of the geometrical forms—a kind of design culture.

Then there was cinema. Whenever people asked his son Federico what his father did, the child answered proudly, "He's a film producer!" He liked going to the set with him and spending time in the cutting room. He would sit quietly in front of the editing machine watching the movement of the film as it danced between the perforated spools. He watched the editor, suddenly grabbing, cutting and splicing the celluloid while tracing mysterious white marks on the film's surface. Each frame was nothing, but all together, one after another, they told stories.

Unshaven, his body swollen, Niccolò kept his eyes shut. He had always been a charming man, always at the center of his circle of friends. He had a sharp gaze, lively eyes, a cocky mustache and ironic smile. His tailor-made suits fitted him perfectly, and he always held himself erect. He had found his own path in the shadow of his father. Cinema had been an adventure. As fate would have it, his last movie was about a kidnapping.

But before that he built a small Ferrari, a vehicle with a one-liter engine which the prestigious car manufacturer had designed in 1958. Niccolò developed the business plan to produce that sports car in series, a vehicle suited for normal streets. The engine had four glowing cylinders with inclined valves, while all four wheels had disc brakes. Bertone had given it its sleek, harmonious design by copying the wind. Production began in the mid-1960s, more or less when his father Oronzio and his uncle Vittorio were fine-tuning the DSA® technology. The car became a cult symbol, much loved by both owners and the drivers who had raced it at Le Mans, Nürburgring and Daytona. Seventy vehicles were produced for collectors, at high costs and modest returns: it was the illusion of a dream.

During the same period, Niccolò had gone to Africa for the first time. Together with

1960s, Oronzio De Nora and his son Niccolò at the Milan office

1960s, Oronzio De Nora and Enzo Ferrari at the performance test of the ASA 1000

1970s, Niccolò De Nora with his inseparable camera

a professional hunter of French origin, he found a stretch of wilderness in the Central African Republic, full of waterways, lush vegetation and free-roaming animals. And then there were the sunsets and the sunrises, with their blinding colors, and air so pure you could hardly breathe it in. This was nature, before the arrival of humans.
His idea had been to build a village and organize exclusive photo safaris. But Bokassa's coup d'état suddenly put an end to that project too: the properties were confiscated and all was lost.
Now, in the darkness of his mind, the last notes of the piece glide by in the background, when Chet Baker lowers his trumpet and starts singing. It only takes the faintest voice to move him, like *Almost Blue*.
Chained to the cot, his motionless body follows the song to the end. Then Niccolò opens his eyes and looks the future squarely in the face. The audience applause was in part for him. If he returned home, he promised, he'd go back to the company. He'd continue the work of his father and take the place that had always been his.

He was freed on 19 June 1978. He kept the promise he'd made to himself and went back to the office, determined to do what he'd never done before. He wasn't a chemist or an engineer but he had what it took to be a manager. He was a motivator, an organizer and a visionary with courage. In the past, the company had belonged to technicians: whoever wasn't an expert kept quiet, and the only expert on everything was Oronzio De Nora. Vittorio was also thoroughly competent, but by this time he was living in America. In 1974 he made the surprise announcement that he had sold all his shares to become a stockholder in Diamond Shamrock, the third largest producer of chlorine and caustic soda in the U.S. after Dow Chemicals and PPG Industries. An article published in the *New York Times* on 18 April 1974 stated that the Italian professor was even in a position to control the American company. But in the course of the interview, Vittorio explained that that was not part of his plans. He thought of himself as an international figure by tradition, and he was only interested in establishing roots in a country that had given him a great deal. "My ties with Diamond Shamrock," he said, "are the result of a love story that evolved into marriage." "I'm a businessman by hobby and a researcher by choice," he added. "Here I want to be a kind of freelancer, so to speak."

ASA 1000 logo

Vittorio was referring to the large plants that De Nora industries had built in America in the 1950s on behalf of Diamond Shamrock, yet he was also thinking of the joint research project that led the two brothers from Altamura to patent the new DSA® electrodes.

As a result, when Niccolò De Nora boarded the plane for Fujisawa, he was alone. His uncle had become a competitor, while his father was old and sick. He felt the burden of responsibility for a company that risked implosion if it failed to grow. He decided to foreground the DSA® anodes as its main product and began working on an ambitious project of taking De Nora industries international.

He also took a walk through one of the parks in Fujisawa to see the cherry blossoms. He wanted to renegotiate the terms of the joint venture established with Mitsui in 1969 and obtain a redistribution of the returns. In the meantime, Japan had become the new beacon of world industry, a model of productive efficiency and technological quality.

Oronzio and Niccolò De Nora with an ASA 1000: the *Ferrarina* produced in the early 1960s in Milan

The beauty of the cherry blossoms overwhelms you. It imbues you with the serenity needed for dealing with the "club of the elect," the small group of elderly stockholders who live on the top floor of the Mitsui skyscraper. Meeting them is like climbing to heaven. But Niccolò had already descended into hell, and he had no fear of heights. He handled the extenuating meetings with lucidity, and he returned to Italy with a new agreement which released funds which had been frozen in Japan. Now he had the resources to begin realizing his project. He understood that in order to sell DSA® anodes to the world he had to go out into the world to produce them. He'd already traveled a lot, and he knew cultures and peoples. He'd probed the depths of human nature and had a detailed map of the planet impressed upon his mind. He'd drawn circles around some places, and one was Brazil.

He'd always had a weakness for the charm of that great country, confident that it would become one of the world's most important. Now it was emerging from the dark years of dictatorship. Niccolò was ready to bet that it would soon become a leading agricultural, industrial and energy producer. He was also connected to Brazil emotionally: he loved the colors, the music and the words of its writers. He had a book by Jorge Amado on his lap, the novelist's first, the one he wrote at the age of nineteen. It was called *The Country of Carnival*, and it seemed to tell Niccolò De Nora's story.

The airplane window framed the sky like a painting, with a patch of sea in the background. This was exactly how the book began: a ship is moving between the blue of the sky and the green of the sea. A young man from Europe is standing on the deck. He frequented the cafés of Paris and spent his time with groups of friends, living on the clever jokes and the vices and virtues of the

The Oronzio De Nora Technologies team for the development of membrane cells in the 1980s

Old World. He's now awaited in a country that moves to the rhythm of samba, populated by cinnamon-colored bodies that give off the scent of parties, their feet following the beat of the music and their fingers grasping the sand. Niccolò lingered over the sentences, slowly, like listening to the sparse notes of jazz. He recalled the subtle cadence of *Summertime* from the trumpet of Miles Davies. It was one of his favorite pieces, a timeless gem from Gershwin's *Porgy and Bess*. He took in fragments of dialogue and brief descriptions of places and people. There was a French girl in a white muslin dress looking out at the sea, while a senator was discussing the price of coffee with a *fazendeiro*.

"Coffee is the wealth of São Paulo and Brazil," he said.

"Of course, it is!" added the senator's wife. "Because Brazil *is* São Paulo!"

São Paulo was exactly where Niccolò was headed. He wished to found a company for the production of DSA® anodes in the city of Cubatão. Seen from abroad, the end to the era of the colonels seemed to be near. Yet the country was still ruled by a rigid protectionist system which made it impossible to invest foreign capital in its production activities. De Nora industries needed to maneuver differently, and Niccolò skillfully managed to reach an agreement directly with the government to establish De Nora do Brasil, which would later move to the industrial area of Sorocaba.

Then came the end of the dictatorship. Twenty years had passed since Field Marshal Branco dissolved the political parties, the period when Niccolò produced the "Ferrarina". It was the beginning of a new era for Brazil, and Niccolò was well placed to take advantage of the new circumstances. He proved himself both an imaginative and concrete manager. From his father he had learned to distinguish between organization and order: he often said that organization is a technical capability, while order is a moral value. In job interviews he would study people's faces to assess their inner strength. He looked for clear thinking and transparency of gestures, characteristics necessary for teamwork, for managing personnel and tackling difficulties. Yet his main quality was his ability to listen, to find the time to hear the views of others. There were people who can create time, knowing that there was always that brief instant before the best decision was reached. His tenacity became exemplary. He never lost focus during technical meetings on topics that were out of his range, and he was always able to listen and look his interlocutors in the eyes to discover their hidden thoughts, just as his father had done.

In the early 1980s, Niccolò continued traveling and drawing new routes on his mental map. In Singapore he walked the streets of a city that seemed like a stage set: colonial-era buildings with wooden façades, plaster ornamentation and brightly-colored doors and windows. Colors, sounds and smells blended together between shop windows and market stalls, while barefoot children splashed in the water of fountains. Niccolò founded a new branch in Singapore in 1982. Then he turned his gaze toward China, and following some initial setbacks, he created the Jiangyin De Nora Tian Li with a local partner, the first step in the development of a group that today is present in Suzhou, Jinan and Shanghai.

De Nora enters the
Asian markets of Japan
and China

Niccolò De Nora
in the pilot's cockpit

De Nora do Brasil,
Sorocaba plant

At the same time, in his capacity as leader of the group, he reached an important agreement with Dow Chemical, with which De Nora industries would develop new membrane cells. In Italy, he concluded a contract with Enichem, a complex and highly structured company which was difficult to penetrate. At the end of the 1980s, he continued to extend his mental map, adding more routes to his plan for international expansion. He focused on India and discovered a profound culture, even in poverty. He met a monk who showed him a dried banana leaf. Written on one side were eight questions: if he answered them, he could turn the leaf over and read his future. He would never be able to read his future, only write it.
In India, he came across a Swedish company that produced matches, with which he established a mixed-capital partnership in Rampur, close to the border with Nepal. Then the world discovered lighters, the Swedish company faced bankruptcy and De Nora Industries were left alone. In 1989, Niccolò traveled to Goa and founded Titanor Components, which was immediately listed on the stock exchange and over the years became De Nora India in the 1990s. He then headed to the U.S., stopping in Paris on the way.

Niccolò's is an exemplary story, one which ends on Christmas Day in the early 1990s, when his private jet landed at the airport in Reggio Calabria. On board was a young lawyer, not Niccolò. It had all started with Vittorio De Nora's move to the United States, when he had become a shareholder in Electrode Corporation, a competitor which made electrodes activated by mixed metal oxides. This production was protected by a patent which prevented the Italian branch of the family from operating on American soil with the same products. But the young lawyer was exploring several promising opportunities, taking advantage of certain details hidden between the lines of the agreement. In particular, he was convinced that not all the DSA® technology was covered by the patent. He was the youngest lawyer of the firm and said things that no one thought possible. Niccolò, though, knew how to listen.
"Are you willing to take this to arbitration?"
"It'll be drawn out and expensive."
"Are you willing?"
"Yes."
These were months laden with tension. Finally, on 24 December, the Paris court of the International Chamber of Commerce ruled that De Nora industries could produce and

Oronzio, Niccolò and Michele De Nora sign the agreement with Dow Chemical

sell metal electrodes based on particular aspects of DSA® technology in the U.S.: a partial waiver that opened up unprecedented scenarios.
On Via Bistolfi, they had been anxiously awaiting the court's verdict, which came on a Christmas Eve which was different from others.
"Now take our plane and go home," Niccolò told him after celebrating the news, almost as if it were an order.
Following that episode, the young lawyer grew together with the company. He oversaw mergers, acquisitions, spinoffs and the founding of new companies. First, he worked by Niccolò's side, then by that of his son Federico and the managers of the group. He undertook a dizzying array of initiatives, each time with the taste of adventure: De Nora style, a mix of intuition, devotion, professional skill, human qualities and commitment to teamwork, placing people above all else.

The last phase of Niccolò's journey was his return home to Europe, after having crossed the world. He now focused on Germany, a country with abundant opportunities and technological resources but somewhat unapproachable, especially for a small Italian multinational. The first step was a joint venture with Jürgen Heraeus's company, which operated in the precious metals sector. After some time, at a seminar organized in Venice in 1998 on the occasion of the 75th anniversary of De Nora industries, Heraeus announced his intention of selling his shares. He wished to restructure his company and no longer considered the sector of mixed metal oxide-clad electrodes as a strategic interest. Niccolò did not hesitate and immediately bought up his shares.
At the time, it was just an intuition. Later, the German company would become the cornerstone of the success of De Nora industries in the new millennium. An international network of research centers, project design companies and manufacturing plants would grow around the axis which connected Germany to Japan. The group would become the world leader not only in the sector of chlorine and caustic soda but also in all electrochemical activities, from the production of the very thin copper layers found in every electronic device to the refinement of metals, from water treatment to the new energy frontier of green hydrogen.
The future was already at hand, at that hotel table in Venice where Jürgen Heraeus was conversing with Niccolò. His sons were next to him: Michele on the right and Fed-

Titanor Components (today, De Nora India), Goa plant, India

erico on the left, in the foreground of the photo. Federico was showing the beginnings of a goatee, which framed a smile that was still timid, youthful and polite. As he looked at the photographer, he too glimpsed the future.

Today Federico De Nora represents the third generation of the family at the head of the company. Oronzio was the founder, Niccolò the manager and Federico the shareholder, the point of reference in an increasingly vast, multinational and complex industrial concern. Over the years, Federico has managed to choose outside professionals capable of embodying the De Nora spirit. He has learned the difficult art of governance, a term which has no equivalent in Italian, a skill that no schools teach.

As Aristotle said, we learn to do the things we have to do by doing them.

1998, Venice Symposium, Niccolò, Michele and Federico De Nora with Jürgen Heraeus

De Nora plant operator
in Rodenbach

DE NORA

EX

Coating system, De Nora
plant Rodenbach

Processing of electrochemical membrane cells, De Nora Rodenbach plant

Growing up

A wooden desk occupied the diagonal axis of the office. It extended with a fluid movement, like a ship's bow. The corners were rounded, the surface coated with a glossy transparent resin and the slats with a dark sealant. It resembled the deck of a sailboat. Federico De Nora placed a coffee cup on the table and stretched out in the armchair. The window behind him recalled a Mondrian painting: the colored tiles followed horizontal and vertical lines to generate an exact meter, an interior rhythm. You couldn't see out the window. The space was cozy, well-lit and devoid of distractions.

Suddenly a ray of sunlight filtered through and illuminated a cloud of suspended dust in the still air of the room. Fine atmospheric particles, no doubt, and perhaps even a mote of cosmic dust. Dust floats through time and tells our stories.

At that time, Federico was the lone head of the family company. The presence of his grandfather and father were perceptible in their absence. Now that they were no longer around, they were always there.

Suddenly the office door opened beyond the ray of dust. Against the backlight appeared his friend Gianfranco Mora, the general manager. Gianfranco had been at Federico's side in the early days at Via Bistolfi and was still helping him find his own way. At the same time, Federico knew he had to discover it by himself.

They sat facing each other, talking about work. The conversation then moved on to memories: Gianfranco recalled something about Niccolò, while Federico thought silently about his father's recent funeral. He remembered the notes of Gershwin playing in the background at the ceremony. His thoughts wandered distractedly through the past. Then he returned to the present. His timing was perfect because Gianfranco was about to tell him something about the future.

"Federico, you're faced with a choice."

"A choice?"

"You can stop here or go beyond. Live off the land or…?

"Or what?"

"Or embark on an adventure."

Gianfranco's ideas about the future were unclear, though he explained that electrochemistry is like an alphabet: once you know the letters, you can make words and sentences and then even write books.

"We could write a book about Grandpa and Dad," said Federico with a smile. "We could start with them and then go beyond—go on an adventure."

That short exchange in the office before a ray of light and the bizarre choreography of dust motes ended on a playful note. Of course, their vision of the future was still uncertain, but at that moment Federico proudly understood the value of inheritance. Oronzio and Niccolò had plowed a furrow in the ground, and now he had to stoop down and extend it. This was what it meant to go beyond: to continue to grow without betraying oneself and one's lega-

▷ Federico De Nora

19 March 1991, Niccolò and Federico De Nora with Oronzio on the occasion of his 92nd birthday

cy, to confirm that the De Nora style was above all a question of people. Federico knew this well, having begun in the early 1990's in the personnel office. A consulting firm had studied the company and called its excessively vertical structure into question. The first working groups were then formed in an effort to share information in a more horizontal and circular manner, to streamline procedures and to think of the company's activities as a set of homogenous and integrated flows. The figure of Operations Manager was created, together with a department in charge of planning, organization and development, headed by Federico. Even then he sensed that his role would be that of strategic regulator. He would delegate authority, without losing control. It was, in fact, a question of personnel: choosing the right people and creating the conditions in which they could give the best of themselves.

After winning the international arbitration case against Electrode Corporation—Vittorio De Nora's American enterprise, which in the meantime had become Eltech—the Italian company became very active in the United States. Scientific research had led to the invention of new coatings, and the Italian electrodes were better than the American ones. Yet the results were still modest. De Nora found itself up against its own colossus, having to compete with its own kin. And then, how could an Italian company beat an American one playing on its own turf? You could try to buy it out, if you had the means, the will and the courage. You also needed to be highly motivated and confident about the future.

Oronzio and Vittorio had invented DSA® anodes and then taken them to the rest of the world. Then they split up, even though they remained brothers to the end. Oronzio's death, though, changed everything: the American company had grown, and the relationship between Niccolò and his uncle Vittorio became strained, conditioned by the seniority and prestige of the professor. The balance changed again upon the death of Vittorio, who left the company to his son Matteo. The old rivalry was softened because Matteo admired Niccolò a lot, both as a person and a manager. He felt close to him, and he understood the difficulties of growing up in the paternal shadow. He appreciated the extent of Niccolò's interests—art, music and cinema. He himself had already cultivated different passions, above all sailing and the America's Cup: Team New Zealand regarded him as more than just a shipowner. Vittorio loved driving a yellow Ferrari, the color of caustic soda; Matteo preferred other colors, such as the blue of the sea. Chlorine and caustic soda were not among his priorities. Federico, then, envisioned the possibility of sitting down with his cousin and joining the two companies, which, after all, had always been one big family.

The acquisition of Eltech took place in 2005. The event signaled the true entry of Industrie De Nora into the United States. It represented the first step in a process

Edinburgh's Forth Road Bridge cathodically protected with Elgard®

Sydney Opera House pillars cathodically protected with Elgard®

of expansion which would lead to a more than tenfold growth of the company in fifteen years. Although Federico couldn't imagine it, his company's development began precisely with that courageous act. It had grown from his decision not to rest on his laurels but to go beyond and explore the new horizons of electrochemistry, from water treatment to green hydrogen. This is how he embarked on an adventure while staying true to himself, his history and his values.

Chlorine and caustic soda went on being the focus of the group's operations, branching into a plethora of applications. Electrochemistry was an alphabet: once you learn the letters, you can build worlds. One of these worlds is the electrolytic protection of reinforced concrete structures, which tend to be corroded by weather and environmental factors. The electrochemical alphabet also contains the solutions for protecting the most impressive manmade constructions.

Cathodic protection of rebar in concrete structures dates back to the 1980s, the result of exclusively Italian research, which De Nora promoted and implemented. The first experimental application took place in 1989 in the context of an overpass on the highway that crosses the Gran Sasso mountain, on which de-icing salts were constantly sprinkled during winter. Humidity and chlorides combined to trigger a process of corrosion. Specific types of cells were installed near the cables and rebar which contained titanium anodes activated by mixed metal oxides. The experiment was very successful and represented the opening page of a new chapter in the book of electrochemistry. From that moment, De Nora developed hundreds of projects around the world to preserve bridges, ports and skyscrapers as well as large, famous buildings, such as the Sydney Opera House.

For the entire month of November, the city was plagued by bad weather. Then a miracle occurred, as if by magic: on 25 November 1996, the sun began shining from the break of dawn, and the southern summer seemed to have finally arrived. The ocean tide at the port retreated, giving way to the human tide that was forming on the quay in front of the Sydney Opera House: over a hundred thousand people gathered before the sails of the building that symbolized the city for the farewell concert of Crowded House, a world-renowned Australian band.

November 2012,
De Nora delegation visiting
Okayama plant in Japan

LIDA® anodes: cathodic protection to prevent corrosion

The excited crowd was unaware that the western walkway had been seriously damaged by corrosion and that only months before a complex operation with cathodic protection had been carried out. The chlorides in the saline environment of the port had gradually eaten away the metal rebar of the reinforced concrete construction. De Nora anodes had made repair work possible by means of a range of current densities in relation to the different types of materials and exposures of the structures. The submerged elements were protected by titanium discs, which were activated by mixed metal oxides lowered directly in the port. It was the first operation of its kind in Australia, covering an area of over 700 square meters.

The Crowded House concert continued well into the night, with a fireworks display and a play of lights on the sails of the Opera House. The musicians left the scene, but Sydney's emblematic performing arts center remained. Thirty months after the operation, the structure was inspected and the tests showed that the system had blocked the corrosion. Ten years later, at the time Industrie De Nora was acquiring Eltech, a new inspection was made. Wherever cathodic protection had been installed, no damage was detected, neither chipping of the concrete nor any form of delamination. Since then, over five hundred thousand De Nora anodes have been installed in more than 30 countries, across an overall surface area of three thousand square kilometers.

Following the Eltech transaction, the De Nora Group was the protagonist of an extraordinary campaign of acquisitions, consolidating its position in the water treatment sector and becoming a leading player in the field of energy. As we have seen, chlorine and caustic soda are still among its main interests: today, Industrie De Nora is the top world producer of electrodes, working alongside industry in multiple markets, from plastic materials to textile fibers, detergents, glass, pharmaceutics, paper, wood and aluminum. The source of all this involvement was the original insight of Oronzio De Nora and the ability of the company's engineers and re-

May 2002, Niccolò, Michele
and Federico De Nora
in front of a portrait
of Oronzio

searchers to master electrolytic reactions. Cathodic protection of immense structures, such as the Sydney Opera House, the *Christ the Redeemer* statue in Rio de Janeiro or the new Louvre Abu Dhabi, represents one of the most interesting application sectors, one which has a significant impact on the lives of people. In the field of component miniaturization, the use of electrolysis has become essential for obtaining the very thin copper layers of printed circuits. These have thicknesses which are sometimes less than a micron and are present in the lithium batteries of smartphones, computers, tablets and electric cars. The core of the production process is still an electrolytic cell; the core of each cell is still the De Nora electrode.

The principle of electrochemical refinement also involves the purification of metals extracted from mines, in particular nickel and cobalt, in addition to copper. The idea is simple: the mineral containing the element to be refined is dissolved in the cell solution; with the passage of the current, pure metal is deposited onto

Membrane plant

2005, Federico De Nora at the Milan research centre on the Via Bistolfi

May 1969, Oronzio and Federico De Nora

29 June 1993, Oronzio, Niccolò, Federico and Michele De Nora, with little Tommaso, in the year of the 70th anniversary of the filing of the first patent

electrodes. The waste is then in part reused and in part discarded.
The first attempts at electrolytic refinement date to the mid-nineteenth century. The introduction of electrodes activated by mixed metal oxides allowed for the improvement of these methods. Yet as Oronzio De Nora taught, scientific research is an ongoing process. The De Nora Group realized new electrodes based on the use of a specific electronic system. While initially the solution was produced by chemistry, now engineering provides the answers. Above all, new electrodes allow lead to be eliminated, a heavy, polluting material. Freeing oneself from the slavery of lead meant the sudden overcoming of a psychological block which had hampered previous generations of researchers. It once appeared irreplaceable, but then the new De Nora electrodes eliminated lead, just as DSA® anodes had eliminated graphite in the 1960s. The key lay in realizing a system of circuits inserted into the electrode structure. The entire component consists of separate segments in which electrified circuits prevent the natural phenomenon of electrochemical corrosion. When copper holds onto the electrode, it tends to tear and perforate it, while lead's natural passivation contrasts this aggressive action. Today, a similar result is achieved by regulating the current in the circuits and controlling the copper's reaction on the electrode. The system is applied to existing coatings, thereby revolutionizing a model that previously had seemed to be crystalized. This innovative solution has launched De Nora technologies onto the industrial scene of the new millennium, where environmental sensitivity in production represents a key added bonus.
Today, De Nora industries celebrates its centenary—an important landmark, full of meaning. Fewer than two decades have passed since Federico took over leadership of the group. Since then, the company has grown more than in the eight previous decades!
Federico decided to try to exceed the ambitions of his grandfather and father: he went on an adventure whose story is worth telling.

125
034
032
075

The De Nora plant,
industrial activation
system, Rodenbach

Activated electrode

Electrochemical cells
for chlor-alkali membrane
technology

The great race

Once again, a clear sky provided the backdrop for the cherry blossoms. The blanched foliage, moved by the wind, resembled the hair of elderly people. The landscape spoke of slower times, the enemy of haste.

A man was walking in a park in Fujisawa; his clothes, height and build singled him out. He was a westerner; everyone smiled at him even though no one knew him. And he smiled back. Once in a while he hinted at a bow. His own rapid, incomplete movements reminded him of the early days of his military service, when he didn't know the ranks and was forced to stand to attention in front of a corporal. He had the impression that all that serenity imbued with perfection was a kind of stage setting, similar to a set for Puccini's opera *Madama Butterfly*. He perceived the tension of latent conflict, hidden behind the inflexible script of ritual gestures and behaviors. But the thought was fleeting, the doubt of an instant.

It was getting warm. The foreigner sat on a bench, took off his jacket and untied his tie. Then he lay down, making sure not to remove his shoes. He fell asleep, using his carefully folded jacket as a pillow. His relaxed hand held his curled up tie on his stomach, which moved with his breathing. Even now passers-by observed him and smiled at him. His name is Paolo Dellachà, and he's the new managing director of the De Nora Group. He arrived immediately after the Lehman Brothers crisis. He's an external manager who was called on to embody the De Nora spirit and values on the ground, like no family member would be able to do. In a word, he's an outsider.

He accepted the position in spite of a distinct sensation of manager fatigue. He had been hoping for some rest in the wake of years of living out of a suitcase, attending meetings in poorly lit rooms, sleeping in hotels that he entered after dark and left before sunrise, alternating between meals on airplanes and award-winning restaurants, drinking aperitifs when he wasn't thirsty and eating meals when he wasn't hungry. This kind of life was full of stress, constantly searching for a free outlet to recharge his phone. Manager fatigue resembles that of the soldier fighting for a cause that's never completely his own. He accepted the position encouraged by Federico De Nora's relaxed smile and reassured by the company's balance sheet. Their solidarity and transparency transmitted a certain idea of calm.

Paolo, the outsider and here also the foreigner, continued to lie on the bench in the Fujisawa park, the same one that Oronzio and Vittorio De Nora had walked through forty years before. In 1969, the brothers from Altamura traveled to Japan to found a joint venture, Permelec Electrode, with Mitsui; now it was the turn of the group's new managing director to participate in the celebrations organized to honor the anniversary. He was still stretched out on the bench, his eyes closed even though he was awake. He thought again about the ceremony that had just taken place in the factory yard. There too he saw cherry trees

Paolo Dellachà in his office in Milan

18 September 2012, the De Nora delegation visiting De Nora Tech for the opening ceremony of the new offices, Ohio, USA

16 May 2017, Paolo Dellachà and Frank Tomaselli at the ground-breaking ceremony for the new plant in Mentor, Ohio, USA

in bloom, traditional costumes worn with nonchalance and glaring light. Then the small bottle of sake was ritually broken, followed by toasts, smiles and bows. Paolo gave a short speech in English, though as no one understood the language, he was speaking to the wind. Still, he chose his words carefully. Even during the celebrations, he had a nagging doubt, like an out-of-tune note, a fissure that destroyed his peace of mind.

Now the sun was hidden behind a cloud and the bench was in shade. Paolo opened his eyes and sat up. Some children were looking at him. He smiled at them and they ran away. Finally, he got to his feet and started walking again, his jacket folded over his arm and his tie in his pocket. He took in the sight of the cherry blossoms, which receded into the distance along the perspective of the avenue. He continued to think, the fissure widening.

Paolo never met Oronzio De Nora, yet like him he possessed the art of asking himself questions. And when questions demand answers, they also end up generating new questions. In Oronzio's mind, that was the course of research. Similarly, Paolo saw it as the idea of development.

Paolo returned to Milan with a specific idea in his head. The first thing he did was to go to Federico De Nora's office, the one with the colored window and the desk on a diagonal.

"I need to ask you something."

"Go ahead."

"Mitsui has fifty thousand employees throughout the world and nearly fifty billion dollars in sales."

"That doesn't sound like a question."

"What use is a joint venture with us to them?"

Federico came into this world with the idea that Permelec was the family jewel. He admitted that he'd never looked at the question from that point of view.

"Good question."

"To my mind they have no use for it."

"What do you mean 'no use'?"

"You're the one who spoke to me about the club of the elect, right? The elderly managers on the top floor of the Mitsui skyscraper?"

"Yes, it was me."

"Do you think any of them knows who we are?"

"Maybe we should ask them."

It was a good answer. They could try to climb their way up the command hierarchy, like salmon swimming upstream. A little at a time, letter by letter, phone call after phone call, then perhaps a trip. They would need to focus on one point: if after forty years Mitsui had never bought up De Nora's fifty per cent, perhaps De Nora could try now to acquire Mitsui's fifty percent. A development strategy was taking shape in the manager's mind.

The first letters were full of smiles and bows in the spaces between the lines, a little like shadow play. Then a few phone calls. They were playing it by ear, without a set plan. At first, they tried to become friendly, then they gently broached the most important questions. The turning point came suddenly, when at the beginning of 2010 the Japanese managers of Permelec and Mitsui asked to

2017, De Nora delegation at the Grand Opening cerimony of the new plant of De Nora China, Suzhou, China

2019, traditional ceremony for the 50th anniversary of De Nora Permelec, Japan

meet the directors of De Nora. A crowded delegation of high-level representatives arrived in Milan. They admitted that Permelec did not play a strategic role in the Mitsui Group and that they might be willing to sell. In fact, they didn't regard the entire electrochemical sector as strategic; for this reason, Mitsui was also planning to sell Chlorine Engineers, the large electrochemical engineering company that it owned in Okayama. Paolo reacted quickly by declaring that De Nora Group would have been interested in acquiring not only Permelec but also Chlorine Engineers. The Japanese shook their heads: evidently the proposal was out of the question because such a large, prestigious company could not be sold to foreigners. That would show a lack of respect toward the country and themselves: it was a question of both image and honor.

The negotiations spilled over outside the meeting rooms. Grappa holds its own with sake, and the Japanese were appreciative. Some started to loosen their ties, while others took off their jackets and rolled up their shirt sleeves. Others again even took off their shoes and stretched out on the hotel couches.

Outside the formal setting, straightforward conversation became possible. It was all about asking questions and understanding the answers. Then they went back to the office and tried to write down what was said or even just mentioned.

Paolo asked for more time: an exclusive contract for several months because without Chlorine Engineers it wasn't even possible to assess Permelec. What was the point of producing electrodes in Japan without the orders of the main client? In a short space of time, the situation seemed to have moved from a smooth normality to the prospect of ending up with everything or nothing. In fact, the Japanese weren't used to signing exclusive agreements. This time it was the Italian company which was making the case a question of honor. They reminded their counterparts of their forty-year relationship and the openhanded dealings of three generations of De Noras. In the end, the group obtained a deal for a few months. The ensuing conversation between Paolo and Federico represented a defining moment. The manager explained the terms of a possible agreement to the shareholder, outlining both the risks and the opportunities. He spoke off the cuff. Once in a while he wrote some numbers on a notepad for future reference. Federico doesn't have his father's tenacious attention; he's more like his grandfather. Many of the older employees noticed the same flashes of light in his eyes that they had seen in Oronzio's: it's in the family genes.

Paolo Dellachà
and Federico De Nora
in Federico's office
in Milan

15 May 2019, Welcome party at De Nora, organised by thyssenkrupp Uhde Chlorine Engineers for the 17th Chlorine Symposium

"So, what shall we do?" Paolo finally asked. Federico had one of those flashes of genius. "Do you feel up to it?"
They looked at each other. No more words were necessary.
And so it came to pass that the new general manager, who wanted to be with his family more, ended up spending more time in Japan than in Italy. He put together a team that was in the know about everything. The offer was prepared without involving consultants. Everything was done at home or while traveling. Paolo didn't hide anything and didn't let different hierarchical roles compromise the intensity of the team's relationships. An efficient, clean operation in the best De Nora style. Oronzio would have approved: that's how he led his own researchers. It would have also pleased Niccolò, who knew how to listen before making a decision.
The important thing was to show the Japanese that De Nora deserved their trust. This was an achievable objective in the rarefied calm of Fujisawa, not far from Tokyo. But Mitsui ordered them to meet with the managers of Chlorine Engineers as well, in faraway Okayama, some 800 kilometers to the south. This was a colossal company, with legions of design engineers and metal workers. In Fujisawa it was difficult to find anyone competent in engineering; in Okayama the president had spent his life manufacturing production plants. He knew the subject front to back, as if it were his life's calling. He resembled a modern-day samurai, with a white strip of hair and the pure metal of a sword forged by the electrodes of an electrolytic cell. In this case as well, it was a question of honor, the valued currency of Japanese culture. In Okayama, foreigners—*gaijin*—were almost completely unknown. They weren't even allowed to enter the city's cafés and bars. The trees were no longer in bloom; the light was faint and dull. Everything was colder though at

Paolo Dellachà in a traditional Japanese kimono

the same time more real: the locals were outwardly hostile and didn't try to mask their displeasure behind rituals of politeness. Over the course of the months, though, the Italians managed to work efficiently—Japanese-style, one might say—weaving a fabric of endless meetings and presentations of joint development programs. By the end, several of their counterparts began inviting them for sake, while some even opened the doors of their homes for dinner. Toward the beginning of the summer, the visitors were convinced that their relationship had changed for the better.

In September 2010, everything finally seemed ready for the definitive signatures. Permelec Electrode and Chlorine Engineers were about to become part of the De Nora Group. Mitsui had only requested—and again it was a matter of pride and honor—that a Japanese delegate stay on the board of directors for a few months. Even when the sale of the companies had been decided, they didn't want to give the impression that a deal had been struck, let alone with foreigners.

All that was missing was the final approval of the club of the elect, Mitsui's elderly shareholders, whom they called the "celestial ones." The Italians decided to spend the last weekend in Tokyo. Another Japanese manager, who had played a key role in the negotiations and had by then become a friend, invited them to his house for dinner. They decided to celebrate with Italian fare and stopped at a downtown supermarket. They wandered through the aisles in search of pasta, tomatoes, mozzarella and wine. Suddenly, the supermarket sirens started sounding at regular intervals; people hurriedly selected their last items and made their way to the checkout counters, quickly but methodically. The Italians didn't notice that the supermarket was emptying out. The sirens continued to sound. At the end, they were the only ones left, the foreigners, their cart full of Japanese versions of Italian foods. The cashier smiled and gestured a bow with a quick movement of her head. The guard at the exit smiled as well. Once in the street, the Italians turned around. They saw the lights of the supermarket go out and the roller shutters come down. It was closing time, yet no one interrupted their shopping: the rhythms of foreigners deserved respect as well.

They arrived at the house, imagining a luxurious home with a large aviary in the garden, cedar trees and a small bamboo grove to ensure privacy. Their Japanese friend, a high-level manager, welcomed them with a relaxed smile into a small urban apartment with rice paper walls. They took off their shoes and began cooking. Then they ate on the floor, with a few camping chairs set out to take the strain off the knees of the westerners. Paolo recounted the episode of several months before when he went up to the top floor of the Mitsui skyscraper to give a short speech that others had already written for him. The circular hallway of that floor—where the "celestial

Milan, June 2022,
Paolo Dellachà and his
team of chief officers

ones" lived—was a large art gallery, with paintings of the greatest Impressionists on the walls: Monet, Manet, Cézanne and Renoir, one lined up next to the other, so close to your eyes that you could touch them with your finger. Then there were works by Picasso, Giacometti and Braque. Immortal pieces for the elect, for the celestial ones. Everyone laughed, especially the Japanese friend.

The following week, the Mitsui shareholders sealed the sales contract with a slight bow. No sooner had Permelec Electrode and Chlorine Engineers become part of the De Nora Group than Paolo was on his way to Germany. The acquisition in Japan meant serious problems back in Europe.

To understand the situation, we must return to the times of Niccolò De Nora and his project to give an international reach to the family business. In Germany he had gone into a joint venture with the thyssenkrupp Group, which in many ways resembled a European version of Permelec, the creation of Niccolò's father Oronzio.

Chlorine Engineers and Uhdenora were, of course, competitors, if not enemies. De Nora found itself in the middle, with its ingenious electrodes activated by mixed metal oxides and its artisanal manufacturing capacity able to realize the projects of its engineers. De Nora was a special company, a catalyzer of chemical reactions between human beings as well.

Paolo Dellachà

Paolo asked Federico if he could use the private jet to get there faster. Sitting back in the comfortable seat of the Falcon, he tried to imagine the reaction of the Germans to the news that the Italians had become owners of the Japanese competitor. It sounded like the beginning of a joke, but there was nothing to laugh about. He would have liked to have a good book on his lap to ease the tension. Instead, he recalled certain passages from *The Art of War*, Sun Tzu's manual: scattered thoughts that enjoy a certain popularity among managers as well, such as "know your enemy, know yourself" or "as fast as the wind, as immovable as the mountain."
Paolo closed his eyes and tried to rest. But he was too tired. Currents of air passed over the Falcon's wings; the Alps were visible below, peeking through the clouds: "as fast as the wind, as immovable as the mountain."
Other phrases from *The Art of War* crowded his mind. One of his favorites is "an invincible defense, a weak attack." He also likes to think of strategy as the art of paradox: "the strong pretend to be weak, the astute ingenuous." Unable to rest, he followed the flow of his thoughts; just before landing he clearly understood that it would all be a matter of transparency. The key to his strategy would be honesty. He'd take his seat at the table and with a certain degree of pride announce that the operation in Japan was a good opportunity and they did well to take advantage of it. Then he'd propose a new agreement. He'd try to convince them that it was possible to realize something new together, something that hadn't ever been seen in the world of alkaline electrolysis, an undertaking that ranged from chlorine and caustic soda to water treatment, from the refinement of metals to the production of green hydrogen.
That was more or less what happened. At first the mood was icy, only becoming warmer with the transparency of his intentions and the simplicity of his gestures. The new project went by the name of *koiné*, a wonderful Greek term to define the language of the world's populations. It provides the words that can be used to name things that belong to all members of the community.
The idea was to create a new joint venture with thyssenkrupp, starting from scratch and pooling all the ownership and knowledge of the two groups. This was a way of joining Europe, China, America and Japan, of taking on people who didn't know each other or even operated against each other and making them work together. The idea was simple and at first glance impossible. Yet as Oronzio De Nora taught, everything new seems impossible.
They had to define the structure of the new company. Yet the truly great hurdle—what at first seemed impossible—was bringing people together. It was necessary to subdivide the companies and create homogenous firms, to divide the research laboratories from the factories and the project design departments from the sales offices. Project by project, country by country, all the companies had to be reorganized on the basis of a new all-encompassing vision, *koinè*, the point of reference for the whole venture.
Created in 2015, today the new company goes by the name of thyssenkrupp nucera. The balance sheet speaks of a successful enterprise worth over three hundred million euros in 2020 and bound to grow significantly over the next few years. The move represented a new leap in scale for De Nora industries, which owns roughly a third. The view from Via Bistolfi is increasingly global.
The new company is a success story for the entire group, which is based on the close involvement of the people who conceived the project and made it possible. These are people who know how to experience emotion in their work and create lasting moments out of nothing. Their contribution is priceless, founded on quality artisanal work: "as fast as the wind, as immovable as the mountain."

An ozone generator

An operator at the Rodenbach plant

DE NORA

Machine-shop work at the
De Nora Rodenbach plant

Machine-shop work at the
De Nora Rodenbach plant

Machine-shop work at the
De Nora Rodenbach plant

Quality control laboratory
at the Rodenbach plant

page 110
Stargard™ Anode

page 111
Anodes for the
electrochlorination
of pools

Anode for cathodic
protection of concrete
structures

Machine-shop work at the
De Nora Rodenbach plant

A pillar of water

The Milanese crowded the downtown streets just before the performance. Some looked for a parking space, while others who lived in the area reached the theater on foot. A taxi stopped in front of the Trussardi shop windows. A young, blonde woman got out. She was wearing high heels and a cashmere overcoat over her dress suit. Her glasses were on her forehead, in her hair. She paid the fare and nimbly sprang onto the crowded sidewalk. She stood still in front of the shop windows and held her ground while passers-by pushed by her. She seemed interested in the clothes, but actually she was looking for the entrance to the restaurant. She noticed the tables of the café and its bright lights shining beyond the mannequins. She found the main door easily and went up to the first floor.

"The De Nora table," she said.

She spoke with a British accent. As a young man, the headwaiter had worked in a pizzeria in Yorkshire and immediately recognized the Midlands inflection with the closed vowels and all the rest. He smiled and accompanied her to a corner of the room which although private was in fact a transparent space composed of glass and reflections. Paolo Dellachà got up. He smiled, shook her hand and offered her a glass of sparkling wine as the introductions began.

The young woman had just been appointed general manager of Severn Trent, one of the largest British companies in the sectors of drinking water distribution and wastewater treatment. She was forty years old, with a brilliant career already behind her. She'd been with British Telecom, where she led operational units with thousands of employees. Interviews with her and cover photos had appeared in numerous magazines in the sector.

To understand the context, we must again return to the past. The connection between Severn Trent and De Nora dates to the final years of Niccolò De Nora's leadership. The British company had shares in an American company that specialized in water purification. Persuaded that that sector would become a strategic one for his company, in 2001 Niccolò created a joint venture with Severn Trent in the U.S. for water treatment by means of electrochemical chlorination. The agreement, however, did not live up to expectations. The De Nora group was the junior partner, limiting its commitment to supplying electrodes.

About a decade later, immediately after the acquisition of Chlorine Engineers, a letter from America arrived at the offices on Via Bistolfi. The sender was a legal firm in Pennsylvania which worked on behalf of nearby Severn Trent. In the meantime, the American partners had created a technological platform called Water Purification, in parallel to the joint venture with De Nora. This was a network of companies, operating in Europe and Asia as well, which supplied a variety of equipment and plants for water treatment, from filtration to disinfection. The lawyers claimed that certain products that De Nora had purchased together with

▷

An electrochlorinator installed in a pool for *in situ* chlorine production

Chlorine Engineers directly competed with them. De Nora took up the dispute, noting that those products were small details compared to the Japanese operation. The Italian company added that it was willing to bring them into the joint venture, on the condition that the American company would share other products in the deal which had been developed through the Severn Trent Water Purification platform.

Negotiations with the Japanese had required months of ceremony; dealings with the Americans got directly to the point. This was business western style: assessing the value of things and transitioning from accusations to stipulating new agreements were both quick processes. The joint venture was redefined and perfected, even though the resulting enterprise was still complex and uneven.

At the time of the creation of the joint venture with thyssenkrupp, Paolo Dellachà and Federico De Nora often spoke about water: they were working on the construc-

Ship with ballast water treatment technology

2019, De Nora team on the occasion of the acquisition of MIOX in Texas, USA

Acqui Terme, Alessandria, Italy, the *Bollente* hot mineral water fountain

Clortec® system, hypochlorite generator

tion of the second pillar of the company, after electrodes: a pillar of water.

They met each week in Federico's office in front of the colored window. They sat at opposite sides of the diagonally placed table, the one which resembled a ship's bow.

"Your father was right," Paolo said. "Water can become the second pillar of the company next to electrodes."

"It's a huge market, which we could conquer one small step at a time."

"There's something I'd like to ask you."

"Go ahead."

"Severn Trent has seven thousand employees in the U.K. and sales of two billion pounds."

"Again, that's not exactly a question."

"Why would they be interested in a joint venture like Water Purification?"

It was a good question.

"We'll have to ask them," Federico suggested.

And so the momentum of events spurred the restless Paolo to organize a meeting with the company's directors. At first everyone thought he was crazy. But once an idea took root in his mind...

The two managing directors were still eating their first course at the table in the Trussardi restaurant, the brainchild of the generously talented Cerea brothers. In the meantime, Piazza della Scala had emptied out, indicating that the performance had probably begun. Paolo had done his homework and read two interviews given by his guest. She held a degree from Cambridge and was a keen soccer fan, Everton was her team. She had two small children and enjoyed running and working out at the gym. He put together this mosaic of details and saw the portrait of a woman with many interests. The interviews further revealed the sense of a mission, one shared by many people who work in the water sector. The woman spoke English quickly, with a cadence that was more abrupt than fluid. Paolo kept close to basics: his sentences were short and well-articulated, his terminology simple and appropriate. Almost imperceptibly—perhaps she herself didn't even notice—the British manager's rhythm slowed down. Words which before were just sounds became sentences. At the end of the dinner, after the last bite and an

elegant touch of her lips with her napkin, she said she needed a few months. She had just arrived and was working on reorganizing the group. She didn't rule out the elimination of some non-strategic sectors. As they departed, they agreed to be in touch.
Over the next months, it became known that the reorganization plan put together at the company's headquarters in Coventry envisioned parting with the American branch which specialized in water purification. De Nora prepared a purchase offer and negotiated boldly, with the result that it acquired a company in a new sector, worth roughly a hundred million euros. The managing director at Severn Trent announced the deal to the press herself: "This sale will allow us to focus on our core activities in the U.K. and abroad, while the water purification sector will become a key part of De Nora's development program."
During the same period, the company on Via Bistolfi purchased an Italian company which specialized in the design and production of ozone generators for disinfection. This was an important addition, as it rounded off De Nora's range of offerings for water treatment. As Paolo stated, "These operations create added value; they allow us to provide a variety of sustainable solutions for our clients and for all those working in the sector. We're building a solid position on the water treatment market, one which strategically complements our work with electrodes."
Nonetheless, the pillar of water was still fragile. The market was very large and fragmented, the competition intense and profit margins often quite limited. The technological platform bought from Severn Trent was excellent from the point of view of designing solutions but lacking in organization. With skill and intelligence, De Nora was able to point to those shortcomings at the bargaining table, enabling it to bring down the purchase price. But now those problems had to be resolved.

In the years that followed, the structure was painstakingly rolled out, and a new corporate architecture was designed in terms of personnel and functions. It was quite similar to what had been done in Japan and China. Federico De Nora personally oversaw the reorganization process, continuing his father's work. Niccolò was ahead of his time in perceiving the development potential of the sector, not only for the company, but for the entire community. Federico was very young at the time and he sat in an armchair next to his father's desk. He watched him work, listened to him explain. He learned the art of vision, which is the first quality of a manager. And so, gradually, water treatment had become more than a business. At the heart of it all was the romantic idea that the purity of water was also the mirror of an inner purity, and that the company's successes were small achievements for the planet.
Federico was now at his home in Acqui Terme, a small town in the Monferrato region that had been an important spa resort in imperial Rome. The aqueduct was a monumental work, a kilometer-long pipeline that collected water from the Bormida River and its tributaries and distributed it to homes, workplaces and production facilities. A widespread water network that brought life and well-being.

Seaclor® electrochlorinator for brine

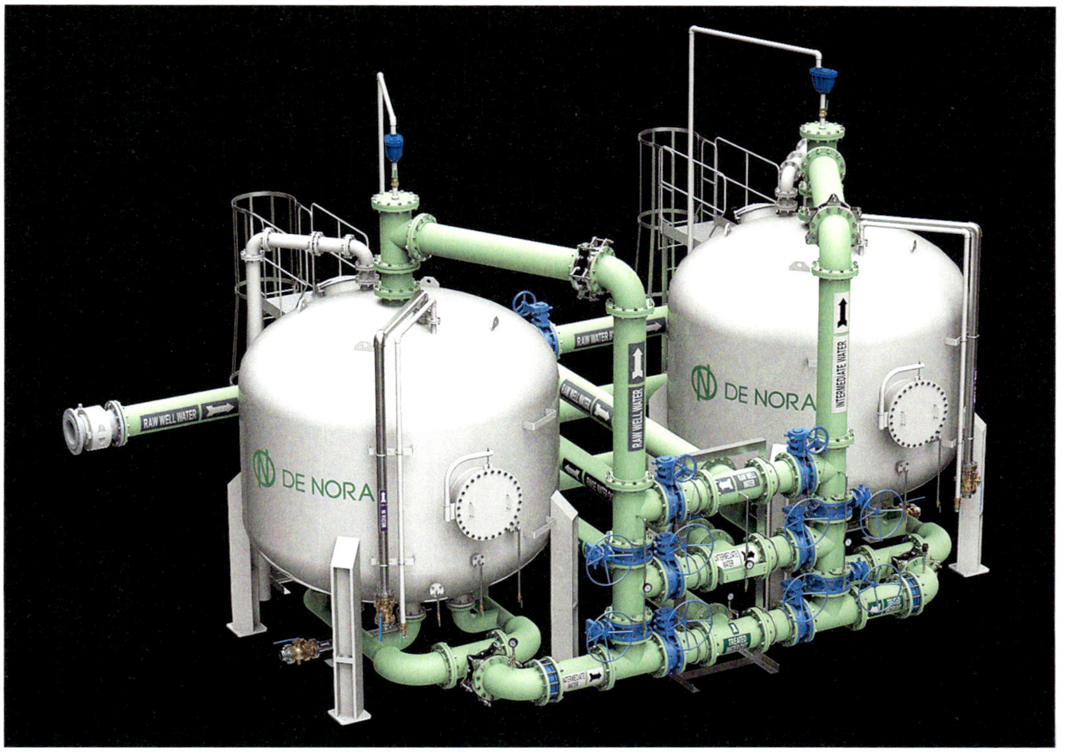

SORB TETRA® inorganics system

Federico was waiting for Paolo Dellachà and a couple of journalists. They chose the form of an interview to talk about water and the prospects for development in the sector. Acqui Terme seemed like the ideal place.

While he was waiting, he listened to some music. He half-closed his eyes and let himself be carried away by the harmonies of his favorite tunes: the jazz he'd learned to love from his father, the funky 1970s, Stevie Wonder, Earth Wind and Fire. He also played guitar; Wes Montgomery and George Benson were the masters he tried to imitate. He never ceased to be amazed at how notes could be juxtaposed in so many unusual ways that they always sounded new.

He took a sip of water from the bottle he kept beside his desk. He sipped it slowly. It was cool. Water is life, as children remind us whenever they play in puddles after the rain, or between the jets of fountains.

When the doorbell rang, Federico was listening to Bill Frisell play a solo. He got up, turned off the music and welcomed his guests. Paolo was wearing a sports top and running shoes. The journalists took off their jackets and undid their ties. The atmosphere immediately became more relaxed, as if the music were still playing in the background.

One of the two journalists was very young. He held his tablet on his lap and took notes by hand, with a digital pen. The older one was a seasoned professional, a science journalist, a writer. He placed the laptop on the table in the study and switched on the tape recorder. Federico filled a jug with water and offered it to them. Everyone accepted and said "thank you": it wasn't often that people drank the very thing that they were talking about.

"Is everything going alright in Hong Kong?" asked the older journalist.

"We're doing an excellent job," replied Paolo Dellachà. "Twenty million citizens are drinking disinfected drinking water thanks to our installations. We've set up a digital system that allows us to have all the parameters under control, in every corner of the city. It's a very sophisticated solution, and it looks like a simple website.

"How important are the digital technologies?"

"We believe in them deeply. They're becoming crucial at all levels: design, presentation, control."

"In a sector that's as old as the world," added the younger journalist.

"The sand filters that we still use today are very similar to the ones that the Romans

used two thousand years ago," said Federico De Nora. "They worked well then too!"
"Apropos of that, De Nora is a hundred years old."
"A century of life. Everything we do began with the intuitive hunches of my grandfather Oronzio, from the time that he invented Amuchina. At the basis of everything is an electrolytic cell: water, salt, electrodes, a current. His legacy is extraordinary and it ties together our research, our products.
"I know you love music. I think I read a statement of yours where you said that in electrochemistry, solutions are like musical notes: they come together and allow you to create harmonies that are always new."
"It's true. Today we have plenty of solutions and we can always offer the best one each time. Each product is an idea, the result of constantly evolving research. We combine technologies: electrolysis, ozone, ultraviolet rays. We disinfect the ballast water of ships, swimming pools, city aqueducts, waste water. Each project requires meticulous and customized work.
"Is that why you call yourself a 'partner of choice'?"
"That phrase embodies our philosophy. It equates problems and solutions, the market and us. In fact, as individuals, any water-related problem affects us all directly."
"How is De Nora Water Technologies structured?" the older journalist asked Paolo Dellachà.
"There are three regional hubs, and Global Business units for disinfection, filtration, electro chlorination and Marine technologies. Some sectors that may seem marginal are growing strongly and steadily. Take swimming pool disinfection, for example. The results for the public are extraordinary compared to traditional chlorine tablets and our market share is now worth one hundred million dollars. Analysts say that the segment is set to grow significantly in the coming years. On the front of disinfection of ballast water from large ships, we're up against very strict legislation. And then technically, it's quite complicated working on hulls in the open sea while the ship is moving. The ship is a floating island. Environmental parameters are constantly changing and the system has to adapt. Each project is a story in itself.
"And tap water?"

Water, the future of the planet

Sentinel® system for UV disinfection of water

“That’s still the great challenge, culturally as well as technologically,” said Federico De Nora. “One-fifth of the world’s population still has no access to clean drinking water. Half of our activities are centered on city aqueducts, as well as the reclamation of waste water.”

“Water as a source of life. And wherever there’s water, there’s De Nora.”

“That’s right, it’s just that not everyone knows it yet.”

Federico De Nora pointed to the journalist’s computer on the table.

“Even without knowing the make of his laptop, I know which processor it has in it. Otherwise you couldn’t be so sure that after switching it off in the evening, you could switch it back on in the morning. Likewise, when we see an electrolytic cell, we know that the electrodes are De Nora. Those same electrodes form the basis of so many of our applications. But not everyone knows that. We’re working on that too. But let me tell you something that is very close to our hearts.”

“Please do.”

“In the water treatment industry, being a leader isn’t simply a question of turnover. It’s also a moral responsibility. It means being able to translate customers’ problems into solutions for the community.

“In the present for the future,” said Paolo Dellachà, in closing.

Meanwhile, the ringing of bells could be heard from outside. The bell tolled twelve times, meaning that it was time for that beloved Italian midday meal. The interview was over. The journalists stood up, said thank you and shook hands with Federico and Paolo. They got into the car and drove through Acqui Terme. They rode past the Bollente, the fountain which still spouts water from very hot springs. Just outside the town they crossed the bridge over the Bormida River. On one side of the river were the baths, on the other the remains of the aqueduct. It was still impressive. The arches looked like spurts of water gushing out of the countryside. A little later they saw a trattoria. The older journalist slowed down and pulled over. He looked at his colleague and smiled.

“Are you hungry?”

“Thirsty.”

“How about a beer?”

DE NORA

Shop floor worker at the
De Nora plant in Rodenbacht

Shop floor worker at the
De Nora plant in Rodenbach

Shop floor worker at the
De Nora plant in Rodenbach

This and following pages
Shop floor workers
at the De Nora plant
in Rodenbach

DE NORA

WURTH

DE NORA

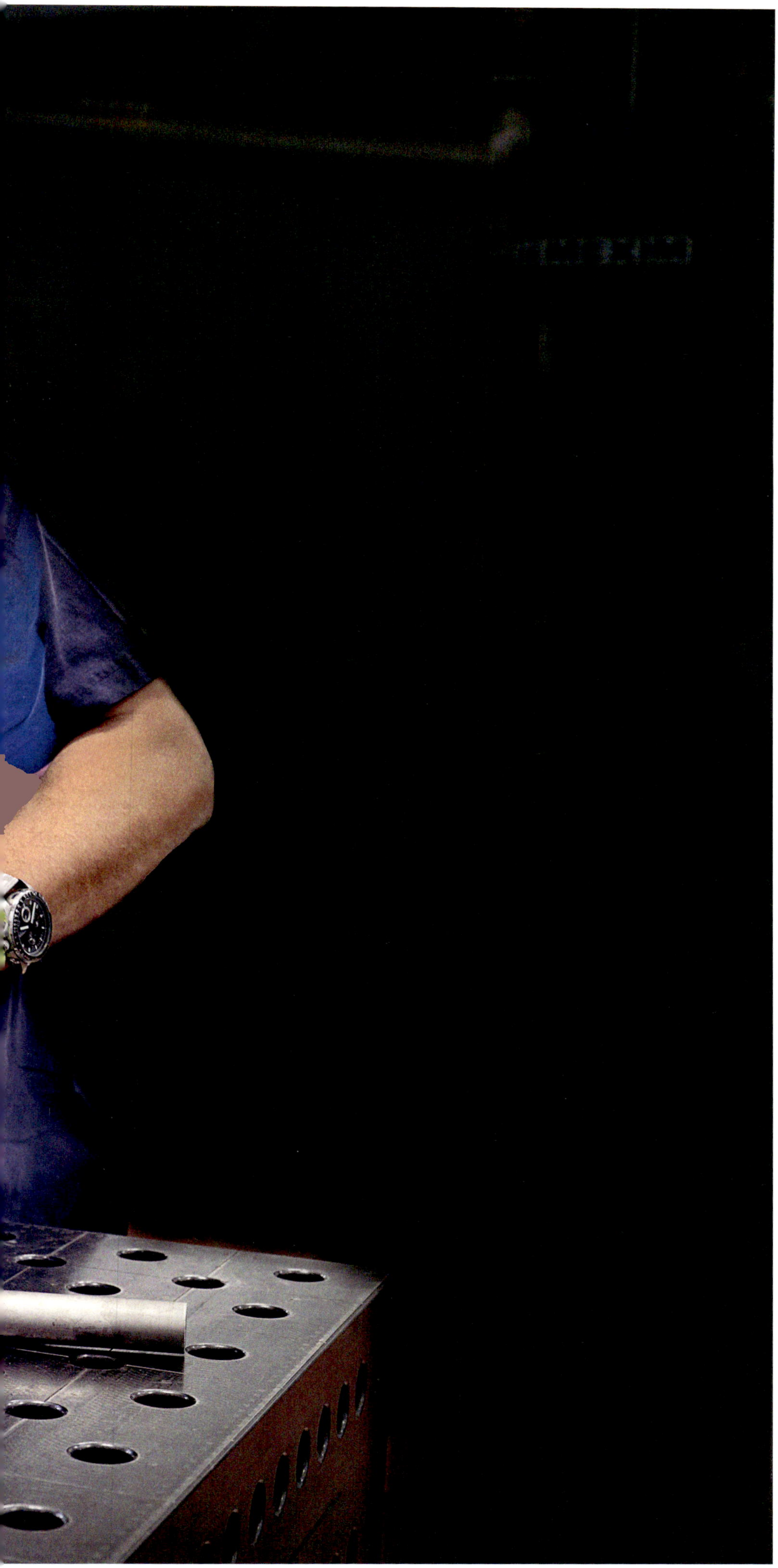

Shop floor worker at the
De Nora plant in Cologno
Monzese, Milan

DE NORA

Technical workers, an
essential asset in De Nora

DE NORA
DE NORA
DE NORA
BORSA

The value of going public

The sky in London was clear, the temperature pleasant. Since early in the morning the British had lined up in front of the polling stations. The population was divided, with some supporting Leave and others Remain. All, though, were certain that history was on their side.

Yet the following day all certainty had gone. Words could not describe the disorientation of the day after, not only in the U.K. but throughout the world. "Amazement" was perhaps the closest label for the prevailing mood.

A look back at the newspapers of that period—it was June 2016—calls to mind those endless soccer matches that we played in the streets as kids. Jackets sufficed for goalposts, and the ball was slightly deflated. Every now and then someone improvised a kick, made more with the shin than the foot. And it would happen that the ball unexpectedly found its way in front of the goalie. Then it might have bounced randomly—deflected, perhaps, off the edge of the sidewalk—and ended up in the goal. The right word to describe something like that was: "Amazement". You could only be amazed at something so unbelievable.

The guy who scored the goal knew he didn't deserve such good luck. Standing motionless in the middle of the field, he would almost feel embarrassed, as if he should incur blame for it. The opponents too would stand around silently, sensing the goal as punishment. Someone would shake his head and murmur, "I can't believe it."

"I can't believe it," Paolo Dellachà murmured, shaking his head. He had gotten up later than usual. He went to the kitchen where he already heard his family talking. Coffee was on the burner, while the radio was talking about Brexit in the background. The catchword was "amazement", although "disorientation" also popped up. He slowly picked up his phone, pausing for some time before sending a long message to Federico De Nora: a time that was consciously drawn out, like a deep breath, following the frenzy of the last months.

The gist of his message was, "I can't believe it." Then he got dressed and left the house, taking the stairs down. In his car he turned on the radio and stopped at every yellow light, though not out of prudence. Rather, he felt doubtful, and also amazed and disoriented.

Stop there or go on? That was precisely the problem now.

A year before, immediately after sealing the agreement with Severn Trent, the De Nora Group began building the company's second pillar. The technological platform for water treatment was reorganized, new research projects were developed and the possibility of further acquisitions was examined. Then, right after summer, the idea of taking the company public gained momentum. The decision was made by the De Nora brothers; it was a difficult one, because it's never easy opening the doors of your home, knowing that you're the guardians of a certain amount of wealth and knowledge

June 2022, Palazzo Mezzanotte, headquarters of Italy's Euronext Stock Exchange - Milan

April 2017, Michele and Federico De Nora sign the agreement with the Blackstone Group

collected over the course of a century and exposing this legacy to the market. Finance and industry are two different worlds, difficult to balance. Yet Federico and Michele De Nora were certain that the company's growth had to be sustained by an expanded base of shareholders to make new operations and acquisitions possible, especially in the water sector. Michele was the finance wizard in the family. For years he led Norfin, De Nora's holding company created by Niccolò in the 1990's to assure stability and development for the economic management of the group. At the time, Franco Mazzucchi was its managing director. He worked next to Niccolò and was very close to the family. Michele began working under Franco, eventually taking control of the holding company himself as Norfin progressively became the strategic beacon of the industrial branch. The De Nora brothers were aiming at diversification, which became the group's watchword.

Going public is like taking a trip: you know when you're leaving, and they tell you when you can expect to arrive; in between there's an adventure that you experience all in a moment. Getting on and off planes becomes second nature, and your home begins to resemble a hotel room. The De Nora managers crisscrossed the world to introduce the company to investors and prepare the terrain for the market. Their strategy foregrounded their electrochemical legacy, the value of electrodes activated by mixed metal oxides, their three hundred-plus patents and their future in the sector of water treatment, a century of history. At least three generations taking their lead from the first intuitions of Oronzio De Nora had managed to create value around the industrial processes of alkaline electrolysis.

They agreed on the date of the company's public debut with CONSOB, the authority which regulates the Italian securities market: 18 July 2016, less than a month after the referendum in the U.K. The entire City and the major newspapers, from the *Times* to the *Guardian*, had come out in favor of Remain. But in the wake of the astonishment and disorientation following the victory of Leave, some thought it wise to postpone the date. The volatility of the markets didn't guarantee the success of the operation. Federico stated diplomatically, "Going public is still our goal; we've just decided to postpone it a while."

So the suitcases were closed back up, as they wished to hold onto the presentations and dossiers. The analysts themselves recommended putting off the operation and trying again in more certain and serene times.

"Two or three years," they said.

"Five or six," thought the De Nora brothers.

Nonetheless, all those frenetic months spent discussing the stock market and finance had created a new culture in the company. The idea gained ground that they could acquire a more relevant public standing and occupy a more significant space. While the attempt to go public suffered a temporary setback, the company still deemed it rational to continue cultivating the prospect of diversifying its shareholder base. For example, they entertained the possibility of accepting a private equity fund as a partner of the group.

In the course of their usual meetings, Federico and Paolo talked about this project as well. They typically met in the mornings, in

30 June 2022, "Bell-Ringing" ceremony at the Milan Stock Exchange

the office with the table placed diagonally and the large window. In spite of everything, the light was calm and the atmosphere relaxed.
"Can I ask you something?" Paolo once said.
"I'm listening."
"Why would a private equity fund that handles billions of dollars be interested in us?"
Federico found no ready answer at hand. Finally he said, "Because we have water. And because we grew without ever going under water!"
Paolo smiled, appreciating the joke.
"Let's try, then, to make it known that we're interested in them, and then we'll see if one of them is interested in us."
He often managed to have the last word.

As soon as the new proposal was put forth, the leading names on the market responded. The De Nora Group had the luxury of choosing the best of the best. Once the agreement was reached, the managers of the American fund Blackstone explained, "In 2012, we launched a platform which today is worth seventeen billion dollars in managed assets; this represents a novel way of doing private equity. We're able to offer our entrepreneurial partners an extraordinary network of contacts on the international level, who can in turn become clients and commercial allies."
The papers gave broad coverage to the new alliance, emphasizing that the American fund had purchased thirty percent of the shares directly from the De Nora family. They called the Milan-based multinational "a leader in sustainable growth technologies." As Federico had foreseen, the company had water and had never gone under. The impression was that it was that

Michele De Nora with his
sons Tommaso and Pietro

sector, which was so closely connected to the future of the planet and to sustainable development, which attracted investors. In fact, few of them knew what an electrolytic cell was and what real growth potential De Nora possessed.
Once the agreement with Blackstone was signed in 2017, it was Federico's turn to ask Paolo a question:
"In your view, will other markets really open up thanks to the fund?"
"Are you asking me if we're going to change?"
"Exactly."
This time Paolo took his time before answering. When he finally did so, his response was precise and lucid:
"We're going to stay the same. But the fund will give us exposure and culture. So, yes, we're going to change."
He often had the last word, which he used with a particular inclination to formulate long, circular thoughts. This was a quality that Federico greatly appreciated.

As we have said, finance and industry are two different worlds. Industry tells stories about people, while a private equity fund is all about numbers, all the way down to those regarding the supply of pods to make coffee in the offices. Control procedures immediately found their way into the smallest details of the company. When it was a matter of introducing the group to prospective investors, the new partners asked that the electrodes for water treatment be removed from the sphere of electrochemistry and placed in that of water.
"But they're electrodes!" Federico exclaimed.
"They're worth more if they're associated with water."
The logic of finance was often obscure. The impression was that communication sometimes tended to take precedence over facts. At the same time, Blackstone brought in a new type of discipline, namely attention to procedures and traceability of operations, which had been missing at De Nora. As

Federico De Nora
with his sons Giacomo
and Niccolò

Paolo duly suspected, participation in the fund did not generate new alliances but gave exposure. And it changed the physiognomy of a company which was growing in the world while staying tenaciously anchored to its historical headquarters on the outskirts of Milan. A thread now connected the neighborhood of Ortica with the posh boardrooms of international finance.

During an interview with Federico, a journalist asked him to explain the reasons for the partnership with Blackstone. In response, Federico emphasized the values of the company culture. He said it was a question of growing, on the inside as well. When things go well for a long time, you don't look at yourself in the mirror. And if your gaze isn't directed outward, you no longer know yourself.

The journalist failed to understand. He took notes, but the logic escaped him, although for Federico it was all crystal clear.

De Nora team on Milan stock exchange on first day of listing

Blackstone's presence had taught them to accept calling their practices into question, to give themselves new rules and to commit to respecting them. The procedures gave rigor to creativity by rendering processes repeatable. Success was achieved one step at a time: you had to change your skin to stay the same. You needed to pay attention to everything, even coffee pods.

In 2020, following three years of partnership, Blackstone sold its shares to Snam, the Italian energy giant that has preserved the dimensions and mentality of a public company. It is run by a dynamic general manager, a great communicator. For some time, it has looked to green hydrogen as the new frontier of clean energy. From De Nora's point of view, passing from Blackstone to Snam was a little like returning home after a long trip. Having absorbed the new regime of procedures, the company now believes it's time to work on investments and to fund development through research and innovation.

Meanwhile, market interest has shifted to green hydrogen. While the world tries to come to terms with the COVID-19 pandemic, many are wondering about the future of the planet and the urgent need to take advantage of new energy sources. A number of players are betting on green hydrogen as one of the main paths toward sustainable development. Today the horizon of hydrogen is upon us. The projects of thyssenkrupp nucera, the electrolytic cells and other industrial products manufactured by De Nora, and the gas pipelines put in place by Snam represent the new paradigms of the energy transition. De Nora is aiming to become the partner of choice of the most important operators at all levels of the sector. In this sense, the partnership with Snam takes on key strategic value.

As it approached its centenary, the company headquartered on Via Bistolfi found it-

self experiencing the emotions of a start-up, even though it had a turnover of more than eight hundred million, employed about two thousand people working in twenty-five locations around the world. What had been a modest multinational was now preparing a new and extraordinary leap of scale.
The experience with Blackstone prepared the terrain; now with Snam the group was ready to go public once again, on the strength of an industrial project that looks to the future. When Oronzio manufactured chlorine and caustic soda, hydrogen was a waste gas that was dispersed into the atmosphere. Today, De Nora is studying new electrodes and cells to enhance the process of green hydrogen production; in so doing, it has given itself a competitive advantage of several years with respect to its main global competitors. With Snam at its side, De Nora is ready to become a global supplier of innovative technologies for the production of clean energy and sustainable growth. Today more than ever, after a century of operations, De Nora's horizon is the future.

Six years after Brexit, then, Paolo Dellachà and the managers of the group again took up the dossiers of the previous initial public offering. They needed to be updated, because in the meantime both the world and the company had changed. Today, the second pillar of water is solid, ready for a new phase of growth, while electrochemistry continues to be the core of the business, with the prospect of green hydrogen launching the industrial group toward a dimension which was unimaginable just a few months ago. Expanding its base of shareholders has become a key strategy for regulating growth. The slogan "diversification" is increasingly relevant. The group needs funds to finance new acquisitions and projects. The perception is that the world's demand for clean energy has suddenly risen exponentially. Water electrolysis, which involves the separation of hydrogen from oxygen atoms by means of electrical currents produced by renewable sources, appears to be the definitive answer to questions linked to sustainable growth, the modern dream of development which creates well-being for the planet and its inhabitants.
On 22 February 2022, a headline in *Sole 24 Ore* announced: "De Nora with Snam: An IPO of $ 5 billion for the Debut of Green Hydrogen on the Stock Exchange." Credit Suisse and Goldman Sachs were managing the transformation of the group into a public entity after exactly a century of operations. De Nora closed its books of the previous year with six hundred and sixteen million euros in sales. The article went on to call the company "a leader in electrochemistry and sustainable technologies."
The group was first listed on 30 June of the same year. From early in the morning, the sun shone brightly on Piazza Affari, Italy's Wall Street. The stairs of Palazzo Mezzanotte provided the backdrop for the group photo, with De Nora banners hanging on the structure's façade. Today the large room where the celebrations took place is silent; and yet its walls speak, conveying the emotions collected over decades of doing business. Federico gave an emotional speech. He spoke of the company's beginnings and recounted how hard his grandfather and father worked to achieve the present result. Paolo took the floor immediately afterwards and addressed his talk to everyone, especially to their colleagues who were following the celebration in real time from the company's branches throughout the world. It was a moving moment, a point of arrival that was also a point of departure. Then the bell sounded. It was nine o'clock on the dot, and the markets were starting to trade De Nora shares. *Forbes* wrote, "Even though it continues to be one of the most important global producers of electrodes, today De Nora has its sights set on water treatment and on the green hydrogen energy transition." The green hydrogen industry is actually an open book whose story remains to be written. One is tempted to say that it's a book of dreams. But dreams are part of reality, the moment before we wake up. "First I dream my paintings," Van Gogh would say, "and then I paint my dreams."

Assembly of an ozone generator at the plant in Cologno Monzese, Milan, Italy

Following pages
Machine-shop work at the De Nora Rodenbach plant

DE NORA
CDDU 981788 3
2,9m 9'6"
45G3
CAUTION 9'6" HIGH CONTAINER

DE NO

Electrochemical cell for
the production of chlorine
from hydrochloric acid

H2
HYDROGEN
ENERGY
STORAGE
H2

The future of energy

The lights go out in the auditorium. Images begin to flow past on the big screen. The first sequence has been shot from above and moves rapidly over a series of mountains and sheer cliffs overlooking the sea, and crystal-clear water of the coral reef. Music, in the background, accompanies the lens as it moves downward between the peaks of rugged, pristine rocks, as old as the world itself. Then comes the desert, its ridges of sand slightly shifted by the wind. High above is the sun.

It looks like nature but is actually a city. The possible vision of a new sustainable world.

Watching the film is like reading a book: *Invisible Cities*, by Italo Calvino. Everything was already there in that book that was such a great favorite of the new generations of architects. The dream, the utopia, the firm conviction that if something could be imagined, it could also be designed. And built.

Marco Polo, the Venetian merchant, would tell the Grand Khan about the cities in his empire. And the emperor listened to him. Through the foreigner's eyes, he saw things he had never seen himself, even though they belonged to him. Invisible cities: cities of memory, of signs, of desire, of exchange. Hidden cities, continuous cities. A tale steeped in oriental aromas, clouds of dust raised by horses' hooves, cart wheels and merchants' footsteps along the silk routes. Yet these were contemporary cities that the young Venetian was describing. They cast long shadows on the screen of the imagination.

Hidden cities, continuous cities. The city in the film is a line measuring one hundred and seventy kilometers and it runs through the province of Tabuk. This is what it is called: the Line. An imaginary line that extends inland from the coral reef between the Red Sea and the Gulf of Aqaba, incorporating mountains, valleys, and deserts. It flows like a river, with no center or periphery, no roads or cars. A place without restrictions, without divisions. A long blank page, like a papyrus scroll on which to write a new chapter of human history.

The infrastructure is underground. The first subterranean level has services and commercial spaces, then on an even lower level is the transport, with fast shuttles running on air cushions. A city powered by green energy, capable of recycling its own waste, making sea water and industrial water potable. A city that was not there. A place of innovation and research, a meeting of peoples and cultures.

The last shot of the film returns to an image from nature. The speaker's mellow voice works with the final notes of the music: "Some will look and see nothing; others will know that this is the beginning of a new way of life". Superimposed on the center of the screen is the Neom logo.

The lights in the Riyadh convention center hall are come up and the audience applauds. A few carefully selected people have been called to represent Neom. A young Arab

Energies of the future

9 December 2021, signing of Neom agreement with thyssenkrupp nucera

engineer comes on stage and takes the microphone. He wears a white tunic, red and white checkered summer headscarf, and sandals. He's not unlike Marco Polo before the Kublai Khan when he explains that the name Neom comes from the Greek Neo, new; he then adds that the final letter is the initial for *Mustaqbal*, which means future in Arabic.

The new future contains The Line and many other projects still under development. Neom embodies a new concept of urbanization, the ambition to govern nature by respecting and preserving it. This region covering almost thirty thousand square kilometers will become an accelerator of human progress: the visionary design of planners, researchers, investors and builders determined to put the fossil fuel age behind them. An old world, like its fuel.

Many of these individuals are there in the hall. There is also the De Nora group, together with thyssenkrupp nucera, because Neom's project is based on the use of green hydrogen as a clean energy source, together with sun, air, and water. More applause in the hall. The enthusiasm of the moment dispels the legitimate doubt that the invisible city is also impossible. But it's interesting that the drive towards a world with no more carbon dioxide emissions comes from a country like Saudi Arabia, which is a major oil producer. It's also interesting that green hydrogen is, to some extent, the harmonious combination of molecules and electrons. The arduous path to the energy transition had created a rift between supporters of electricity and defenders of fossil fuels. The electrolytic cell has both: electrons convert water into oxygen and hydrogen molecules, creating gas. Seeing the images of the city of Neom, so perfectly integrated into nature that it is invisible, inspires the romantic idea that there is a balance in the mystery of the universe. A truth that had remained hidden until the planet was nearing its end, only to suddenly reveal itself and allow for a rebirth, thanks to scientific research and technological progress. The circular idea that problems already contain solutions. A perfect narrative structure.

The young Arab on stage announces that Neom will be an autonomous region. He looks at the Westerners in the room and adds that the area will be the size of Sicily or Belgium: an archipelago of settlements conceived as a series of mutually related communities. Ports, industrial areas, residential districts, laboratories, research centers, human-scale technologies that will free up more time in life. The first cognitive city, where machines adapt to human needs and technology learns to anticipate them.

An invisible city, the engineer concludes, enclosed in nature like a yet-to-be sculpted piece contained in the marble. Applause.

It was the end of February 2020. Two years after the presentation of the dream, De Nora and thyssenkrupp nucera signed the contract for the supply of more than thirty thousand electrolytic cells within a complete plant for the production of green hydrogen. It was to be installed in Oxagon, the floating city that will be Neom's industrial lung. A century later, De Nora's electrodes assist in the possible rebirth of the world. The foundation stone of the invisible city.
Exactly twenty years have passed since Jeremy Rifkin published his book on the hydrogen economy. His ideas began with the consideration that in the history of mankind, the rise and fall of civilizations had always been connected to the availability of energy, to the ability of only a very few to produce it in order to distribute it to many. At the dawn of the third millennium, Rifkin had glimpses of the future by imagining a new world order based on a different energy economy. It was green hydrogen, obtained through the electrolytic decomposition of water, according to a model inspired by the internet and the way internet content is spread. A new form of democracy where each user can be both producer and consumer. Opportunities would be redistributed in favor of the global south, with its wealth of sun and wind capable of producing clean electricity at competitive costs. A kind of redemption of the less fortunate populations.
In the last twenty years, the desire to cleanse the atmosphere of carbon dioxide emissions has become a necessity. The cost of producing green energy has come down and research into hydrogen continues. It is the most widespread element in the universe: stars are made of hydrogen, the sun is a mass of hydrogen, ten per cent of our body is hydrogen. This molecule is very small, light, and volatile; on earth it is only found combined with other elements, such as oxygen in the water molecule. It is so small that it tends to elude us and yet it can save the world.
It's not hard to imagine a future in which green hydrogen plays a major role in the global energy supply. There are those who envisage producing it in the most cost-effective parts of the planet and then distributing it where it is needed in the quantities needed. In this sense, existing gas pipelines could be used, at least partially, for transport. But it could also be compressed and moved by land or sea, in the form of green ammonia - essential for producing fertilizer, among other things. Many are ready to bet that Italy could play a decisive role in the hydrogen routes between north and south, east and west. In the center of the Mediterranean, at the heart of trade. The tiny hydrogen molecule could also be stored in the depleted gas fields in our country. Enrico Mattei, the head of Eni, had discovered and exploited them after the war to give Italy some independence in terms of energy; today they are natural available underground storage spaces.
In any case, it will be a new leap in scale for De Nora industries, towards ever more complex frontiers. The company will have to set up veritable factories to build new electrolyzers in the most diverse parts of the world, recruiting workers who can enshrine the De Nora spirit and values, and

NEOM Green Hydrogen Company production site under construction in Saudi Arabia

Opposite
Rendering of the new giga-factory in Cernusco sul Naviglio, Milan, Italy by Stefano Menotti Colucci & Partners

rapidly acquire skills honed over a century of experience. As always, the key to this expansion process will be research and the development of talent, dialogue, listening and training. The green hydrogen sector is at the dawn of a long period of growth. There will be great interest in this market due to the scale of the investments. Goldman Sachs has estimated that, to build the infrastructure needed to decarbonize the earth, more than fifty trillion dollars will be required. De Nora will be there, with a century more of history than anyone else.

Jules Verne wrote this in the nineteenth century, the century of coal: "Water will one day be a fuel. Hydrogen and oxygen will provide heat and light." The book was *The Mysterious Island*, and the year was 1874.

If the dream of the new hydrogen economy is beginning to come true today, it is also thanks to De Nora's research. Oronzio's legacy is being passed on to new generations. On the one hand, the capacity to produce electricity from renewable sources has improved, and on the other, the costs of electrolyzers have come down and plants are increasingly more efficient. Since the early anodes activated with mixed metal oxides and the first cell diaphragms and membranes made by Oronzio and Vittorio De Nora, today the key to research is in engineering. The Director of the Group's Re-

Dragonfly® system, internal stacks

Dragonfly®, innovative electrolyzer for the production of green hydrogen

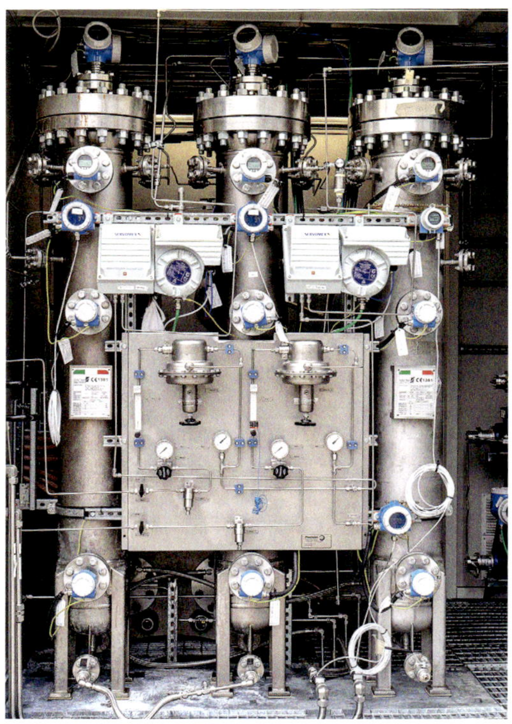

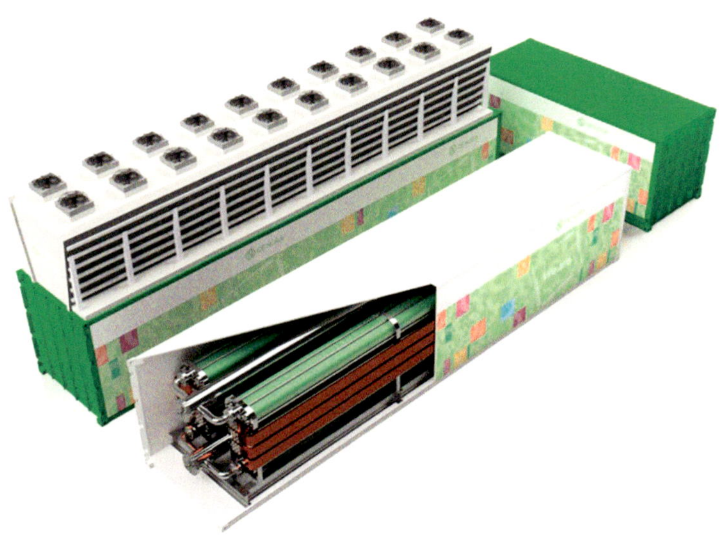

search and Development department calls it "an inexhaustible source of solutions for electrochemistry". A blank page — like Neom's project — on which to write the future of alkaline electrolysis.

Over the past three years, the company has invested seventy per cent of its research resources in green hydrogen, accelerating the move towards the energy transition. There is still much to be done, but the results are already concrete. The road ahead is still long: it will be at least a couple of decades before we can switch from oil, coal and natural gas to clean energy. From this perspective, the solution will not be a single source of clean energy, but a combination of strategies. De Nora will be a key player on all fronts, with its innate flexibility, patents, and experience gained over a hundred years. Wherever there is a need for green hydrogen, De Nora technologies will be there. Efficient, low-cost electrolyzers, made with the most advanced technology and quality craftsmanship, of every size, in every part of the world. The first 33,000 units are already on their way to Oxagon, the region of Neom, Saudi Arabia.

The lights go out in the hall. On the big screen, images begin to roll past. The first sequence has been shot from above, and shows the sun shining on a long stretch of desert coastline, rugged rocks, mountains as old as the world, sheer cliffs dropping into the sea, and the crystal-clear water of the coral reef. On the surface is the largest floating industrial complex on the planet. An octagon, at the top of the Line.

The city of Oxagon is criss-crossed by a maze of canals, like Marco Polo's Venice, but a millennium later. There will be the most innovative industries, research laboratories, study and training centers, an immense fully automated port, and facing the trade routes, vertical hydroponic greenhouses, digital technologies and artificial intelligence, and an oceanographic institute for the preservation of the underwater environment. The speaker's mellow voice works with the last notes of the music, saying: "This is the place where ideas can change the world. This is Oxagon."

The lights in the hall come up. The audience in the Riyadh Convention Centre applauds. The foundation stone of Neom is Oxagon; the foundation stone of Oxagon is a De Nora electrolyzer for the production of green hydrogen.

Everything has yet to begin, but for the De Nora group, the future is already in present tense. Applause.

This and following pages
Machine-shop work at the
De Nora Rodenbach plant

uvex
uvex

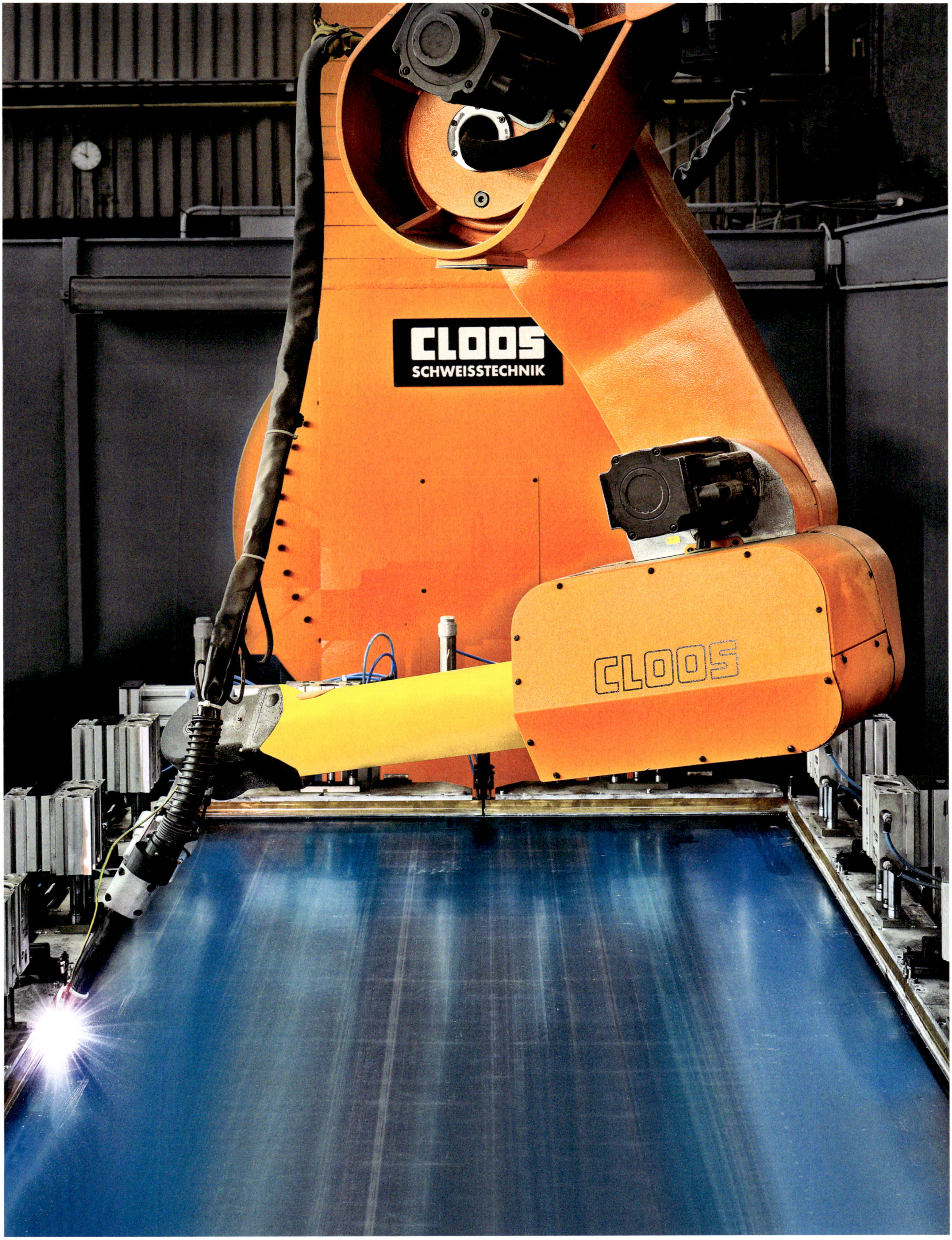
CLOOS
SCHWEISSTECHNIK
CLOOS

Machine-shop work at the
De Nora Rodenbach plant

EX

Machine-shop work at the
De Nora Rodenbach plant

People, at the heart of the enterprise

The street is deserted, it's early autumn and promises to be cold. Illnesses will be on the rise with the cold weather. Lombardy is in the red zone again. Milan seems to be the epicenter of the pandemic. On the corner of Via Bistolfi is an army truck. A hefty sergeant steps towards the middle of the street and raises his arm. The car slows down and pulls over. The driver lowers the volume of the radio. He was listening to the news.
"Good morning," says the sergeant.
"Good morning."
"Where are you going?"
"To work, to the office."
"Do you have your self-certification?"
"Yes, I do."
The man opens the glove compartment and takes out a bundle of papers. He rifles through them quickly and picks one. He adds the date and hands it to the soldier.
"Do you have another document?"
"Yes, of course."
The man takes his wallet out of his jacket pocket and pulls out his ID card. He hands it to the soldier. The sergeant takes a quick look, then goes off towards the truck. The man behind the wheel watches him. He sees him talking on the phone. His instinct tells him to turn up the volume on the radio to hear the end of the news. Instead, he stays there, staring at the sergeant. He imagines he's checking the documents, cross-referencing data, trying his best to obey the rules. In the face of complexity, over-simplifying a rule often seems inadequate. However, the rule is also the expression of a strategy: the synthesis of clear thinking aimed at solving a problem. Isn't the lack of rules proof of a lack of thought?
Thoughts chase each other in the mind of man. They go beyond the pandemic to his company, to the urgency of the tasks at hand.
The sergeant comes back and hands him the document.
"There you go. Have a good day."
"Thank you. And you have a good day."
The Director of Human Resources of the De Nora Group starts his car again. The engine revs. First, second, third and he's already there. He flicks the turn signal. From the street corner, the sergeant watches him as he drives into the factory yard. Meanwhile another car approaches the intersection; he raises his arm, and it stops.

The meeting room is on the upper floor, with the glass window and terrace. The large table allows for safe distances. There's a microphone with an amplifier in the middle and a large monitor on the wall.
Some colleagues are already sitting while others are arriving. The HR manager greets everyone, makes some coffee, switches on the monitor and goes online. Gradually, the faces of the group's directors from around the world appear on the screen.

Milan Ortica District, Federico De Nora in front of the mural dedicated to his grandfather Oronzio

2705
VIA
ORONZIO DE NORA
INGEGNERE INDUSTRIALE 1899 - 1995
(GIA' VIA CARARCO)

24 June 2021, Milan, unveiling of street sign for the Via Oronzio De Nora

Work team for the realization of the Via Oronzio De Nora

Top management is meeting to discuss the company's *Vision*. They want to write one sentence that encapsulates everything. The horizon of a multinational industrial group looking to the future after a century of business. The *koinè* of the joint venture with thyssenkrupp comes to mind: the language of the people.

When he speaks, the director instinctively lowers his mask, then raises it again.

"I wanted to thank you for accepting the invitation. It means a lot. First, I'd like to draw your attention to the concept of loneliness. More precisely: the loneliness of the word. We human beings are condemned to exchange words one at a time. We think in parallels, but we speak in series. Today, the task is to find the exact words to compose a sentence. A single sentence that says who we are and who we want to be. This is no small feat."

One of them immediately looks up from the documents he was reading, interested in the solitude of the word.

The work continues throughout the day and everyone makes a generous contribution. An external advisor guides them through the development of the concept and at the end they write the sentence. A few solitary words, one after the other, clearly expressing the precise vision of the De Nora group.

It was thought up in English, because this is the language they use to cross borders. A phrase conceived by a collective intelligence. In the end it sounds like this: *leverage available talents as catalysts for a sustainable future*.

It means that De Nora is committed to enhancing and promoting all available talents as catalysts, sparks of a sustainable future. In the electrochemical world, the catalyst is a bit like the myth for historians or the etymon for linguists. The catalyst causes chemical reactions, regulates energy levels and allows reactants to combine with each other. It is one of those technical words that seems to be made for becoming a metaphor. De Nora likes to think of itself as a catalyst for processes. The catalyst's destiny is to get in the way: to listen, understand, solve. At the end of the day, whatever phrase the team came up with, the word catalyst would probably have been there.

Then there is the call to the future, perhaps somewhat taken for granted these days, especially in the sustainable version. But that, too, has been part of De Nora's genetic code, ever since Oronzio's first tilted electrode cells. When he cut himself and

Graziano Marcuccio
in his office in Milan

dipped his finger in the brine of the electrolyzer, he imagined the future. We would realize this a century later, during the pandemic, constantly washing our hands with his Amuchina. Today, De Nora's technologies are all about protecting the environment, from green hydrogen production to water treatment. Whatever phrase the team came up with, the hint of a sustainable future would have been there.

The great innovation that distinguishes the De Nora vision is the first part of the sentence: Leverage available talents. It means that the company's assets are its people. All talented, but each in a different way. The mission is to seek them out, find them, help them to give the best of themselves. Not for themselves, but for the community.

A few years earlier, the HR department had also worked on a first *People Strategy*. The company lacked a *People Strategy*. There was no lack of documents specifying everyone's tasks and duties. What was missing was a reflection on individual and collective value, on what the organization expected from each person and what each person could expect from the organization. The HR director called several meetings with managers, employee groups and department heads. He had specifically focused on the topic of talent, to understand what it is, how to recognize it, protect it, and develop it over time. They realized that talent is first and foremost an investment. They had imagined it as a verb, transitive, conjugated in the future tense. Talent expresses an action that is often hidden, hard to recognize. Everyone has a talent, but it must be uncovered and polished like a precious stone until it begins to gleam.

In the field of electrochemical research, De Nora has always been a talent factory. Some researchers in the group are true geniuses—like Oronzio De Nora. But the problem is developing group talent. As if talent were not the gift of a single person, but the sum of the micro particles that make it up. It is precisely those fragments of an individual that join other fragments of other individuals: collective talent as a binding of molecules, in a chemical reaction.

Finally, strategic thinking had been developed based on keywords that encapsulated universes of shared values. It was a complex task, which translated into projects, successful initiatives and results to build on. After developing the *Vision*, it was time to start again. The North Star to follow was even clearer now. The second *People Strategy* was based on five pillars: Development, Diversity Equity and Inclusion, Well-being, Digitalization, Reputation.

That work was later synthesized in a video that presented the strategy to employees, and the company's essence to new recruits; a short-animated film with simple drawings, graphic lines and rich, elegant, unshaded colors. It shows a balanced world full of flowers and plants, where people grow by helping each other, climbing ladders and reaching the top, each following their own path. Listening to everyone, but especially to themselves; cultivating their passions. Believing in the talents of individuals also means realizing the company could lose them. In fact, the video ends with the image of a leaf falling from the plant and fluttering away. The voice-over says: "If your dreams take you far away from us one day, we hope that everything you've learnt at De Nora will help you to shine, following the values that have made us great together."

The work—a bit like a relay between *People Strategy* and *Vision*—created a more intense dialogue between the different personnel levels, integrating different points of view, ideas and perspectives into a single, shared thought. Nothing was lost from that work. Similar to a piece of literature, in addition to the text that goes to press, there is a wealth of valuable material left over. Thoughts, fragments of discussions, letters, notes. The solitude of the word. The human brain being condemned to think in parallels and express itself in series: one letter after another, word by word, from beginning to end.

The HR manager likes to collect those phrases that spontaneously come from everyday life in the company. They are an inexhaustible reserve of ideas. Good ideas. They are also stories; portraits, so to speak. People are stories. Knowing how to listen to them already means recognizing their talents.

At a later date, an email notification pops up on his computer screen. The HR manager reads it, smiles, prints it out. He also wants to add that text to his collection of words. "It's great when things that you've thought about become reality. And really satisfying when you see those things appreciated and used by the community." There's also a photo in the message, taken with a phone from the office window. It shows the street next to the De Nora office seen from above, with plants and benches, colors, murals, picnic and ping-pong tables. A group of young people can also be seen in the photo. They're studying.

What was once an old abandoned street in the Ortica district has been turned into a

pedestrian area, a kind of piazza. A street that becomes a piazza already contains an idea of community; a space designed to welcome people. De Nora developed a project that had been approved by the Municipality and supported by Municipality 3 and the neighborhood associations. Then street furnishings were added, with the idea of a safe place for everyone. And the wall bordering Industrie De Nora had been painted with a series of murals revolving around science. Strong graphic images, with portraits of great researchers: a gallery of those figures who contributed to the development of humanity through scientific research. Alongside Natta, Veronesi, Golgi, Forlanini, Cristoforetti and many others is Oronzio De Nora, after whom the street is named. The last face belongs to an anonymous researcher. But actually, it's a symbol. An idea of the future. In the white space of that face are all the students who have yet to become researchers, together with generations of scientists who stayed in the shadows of their laboratories, illuminated by the light of passion.
That new street in Milan is the place that Oronzio De Nora would always have wanted. It expresses all his love for young people, his conception of study as nourishment for the mind and soul. But also, his joy of life, his tendency to cultivate curiosity, interest, and wonder.
On 24 June 2021, still stifled by the pandemic, a meter's distance between each person and wearing masks, the inauguration ceremony was held. There were city authorities and association representatives. There were De Nora employees and many ordinary people. Federico gave a beautiful speech. A few words from his heart. He spoke about his grandfather, who had died at over ninety years of age without ever getting old. A man with an unshakeable faith in the new generations, who had established awards and scholarships to provide jobs and training for new graduates. He devoted his entire life to building a bridge between the worlds of university and work. A commitment that has remained unchanged even today, in the multinational De Nora group.
Federico also spoke of Oronzio's bond with Milan and the Ortica district. He ended his speech with the words his grandfather used to repeat to them as boys to encourage them to pursue their dreams: "I've never worked a day in my life, because I've always done the thing I loved!"
There's a lot of De Nora spirit in this new street in Milan: Via Oronzio De Nora. Painted on the walls, hovering in the air. There's the past, which in the present looks to the future.

At the end of the day, the HR manager collects his pages of notes. He spreads them out again on the office table, to look at them all together. Like a group photo. Some are handwritten, others printed on cut or torn pieces of paper; then there are fragments of interviews, quotations from press releases. A wealth of thoughts formulated by Federico, Paolo, Christian, Alberto, Graziano, Andrea, Lorenzo, Paola, Barbara and many others, who work and identify with the De Nora world. There's enough there to fill a book. Phrases about the culture of the mistake, responsibilities, the value of dialogue, humility, the ability to govern time. And there's more: about listening, rules, the harmony of the group. Phrases such as: "Rules must always serve the ends, never be the ends unto themselves". Or: "The mistake is the first step on a path to possibility. Without the mistake there is no path and nothing becomes possible".
He really likes a thought about the harmony of the group. He says: "We are weavers of human relationships. We weave relationships between people. We combine different fabrics and sew tailor-made clothes that dress the personality of the wearer. Rules are clothes too. You think about them, discuss them, share them. When you wear them, they are a second skin. Really, someone ought to write a book with all

Christian Urgeghe at the Milan research center

those sentences scattered about, like a chorus of lonely voices.

Before the day ends, he reads one more. It regards the future: “The minute we think about it, the future is already in the present. Living in it will be a wonderful enterprise, because we have people at the heart of the enterprise.”

He smiles. Satisfied. Then he stuffs everything into a folder that he closes with an elastic band, being careful not to crumple the edges. Finally, he chooses a felt-tip pen and in a beautiful hand, writes in block letters on the cover:

PEOPLE, AT THE HEART OF THE ENTERPRISE.

He puts the lid on the marker and puts it back in the drawer.

The folder, on the other hand, he leaves on the table. On top of everything where it’s always in sight. *People, at the heart of the enterprise*.

Milan office, hallway with mural depicting De Nora staff at work, by Anna Ramunni

H2

Milan, Via Oronzio De Nora, mural dedicated to Women and Men of Science, a project created by Ortica Noodles

De Nora 50th Anniversary Manifesto: De Nora was ahead of its time with hydrogen generation and water treatment technologies already in our portfolio in 1973

Our 50th year in the design and contruction of electrochemical plants complete systems and equipments for the production of:
chlor-akali and derivatives - hydrogen and oxygen - hydrogen peroxide and persalts - fatty alcohols and detergents ammonia and fertilizers - sulphuric acid - water purification and exhausted gases plants

ORONZIO DE NORA
IMPIANTI ELETTROCHIMICI S.p.A.
Milano - via Bistolfi, 35 - telef. 23.94 - telex 31.552
Il nostro
50°
anno
nella progettazione
e costruzione di
Impianti Elettrochimici
impianti completi e macchinari per la produzione di:
• CLORO-SODA E DERIVATI • IDROGENO E OSSIGENO • ACQUA OSSIGENATA E PERSALI • ALCOLI GRASSI E DETERGENTI • AMMONIACA E FERTILIZZANTI • ACIDO SOLFORICO • IMPIANTI PURIFICAZIONE ACQUA E GAS DI SCARICO.

Image for the Centenary,
by Stefano Pietramala

100 DE NORA
since 1923

DE NORA